Damaged God for sale

82 devoted ponderings

By Russ Duket

This book is not intended to be viewed or used as anything other than a collection of my personal experiences and how I made sense of them in my walk with Jesus. I do not claim any special insight or anointing from God on any topic. These are my own personal devoted ponderings.

All scripture quotations taken from the King James Bible, the New Living Translation or the New International Version.

This paperback is a re-edited version of the Kindle version. We found some mistakes and fixed them. The heart is the same, but the punctuation and grammar are better.

Introduction

My name is Russ and I've had over 30 years of serving in Children's Ministry and it probably shows by the way I think. (*I hope that works for you*). I also spent several years in a church that used the Word of God in a way that I found to be controlling and judgmental. It wasn't all bad. I met many great people, learned a lot of solid Bible doctrine and had numerous wonderful experiences there, but for me, the Word has to look like Jesus. I hope that will explain the way I communicate. God generously led me to children's ministry so I could teach the way I need to be taught, with sock-puppets and cookies and prop-filled object lessons. I apologize if I avoid the usual preaching tools and stick with what works for me. (*I have a hunch that there are more grown ups out there who need sock-puppets*)

Most devotionals are arranged in order with themes and dates corresponding to the calendar. This is not one of those. I would rather write 80 pages of things I think God shared with me or taught me, than a 12-month devotional of religious cliché's, more full of stale air, than Holy Spirit. I realize there are a lot of *'what if'* ideas in here, but God frequently speaks to me that way. These were written during a unique three- year chapter of my life and they are not in chronological order. They are called "Devoted Ponderings", and I mean no disrespect. I know God is Holy and above everything, but He is also intimate, meets us where we are at and is closer than our own families.

I kind of picture it this way: Sometimes, I push open the door to His den and interrupt Him to ask a question or two. He puts down his pen and closes His notebook to give me His undivided attention. Other times, He approaches me and invites me to go with Him for a ride. We load up the car and roll down the windows. He starts talking about stuff and asks me questions to get me to think. Sometimes the questions get me to think differently about myself and others. Sometimes the questions get me to think differently about Him. In both cases, I love talking to my Dad. He is so smart and so cool. I want to be like Him when I grow up!

These writings are merely a part of my journey and I am inviting you into those conversations I've had with my 'Dad'. So what is this book for? That'll be between you and God. I don't think God has a lot of strict rules on us spending some time in His den or on a mental road trip with Him. "*I am convinced*," as Paul said, that God really loves it when we choose to spend time with Him. You will also find reoccurring themes in here. God often has to paint me a few different pictures of the same lesson, (*over and over and over*), before it gets firmly planted in my heart, mind and spirit. I celebrate His patience and creativity!!!

You will definitely notice that I don't use verses to back up everything I say. I see Jesus as the embodiment of scripture, the correct interpretation in fact, so I'm just sharing what I've gotten from my Jesus (*any miss interpretations you find, I apologize for in advance*). I'm not into believing that I can have special Bible revelations, extra wisdom or that I should start throwing verses around at people. *I saw first hand the hurts they can inflict when mishandled, so I tend to avoid that.* I do believe the Bible is the inspired Word of God. I'd just rather it be the Holy Spirit who wields it, than me thrashing around with it. So then, why do I use the King James Version when I do quote scripture? *Good question.* I actually find it easier to memorize than a common language version. It makes it sound like a cool movie quote to me. I also use KJV because the 'religious sound' reminds me to look for the kind heart behind it, instead of the hammer of the law.

A lot of my thoughts and leadings come from the pictures that verses paint in my head and I also noticed that the only time Jesus was adamant about quoting scripture was when He was resisting the devil or taking a stand against the legalistic religious crowd. He often skipped the preaching to the folks He met and went straight to imparting understanding and wisdom (*the whole reason for the scriptures anyway*).

I am not the best anything. I am also not the worst. Man, son, husband, father, friend, worker, disciple, teacher, artist... neither best, nor worst. You may find me taking too much blame on one topic and not enough on the next, I am broken in as many places as everybody else and these are just my notes, revelations and stories from the journey through my brokenness. You will also find some things that make you ask, "*Is this Russ guy ok?*"
I have had many broken places at my own hands. I hope that I am never "ok". Jesus didn't die for me to be "ok." He died for me to be a wondrous anomaly to the world around me (*and even to myself at times*). So I'm aiming at that instead!

Just a warning, some topics in this book may confuse, some may convict, some may bore and some may inspire.

I am hoping for more of the last option, than the other 3.

Hugs and thank you for reading this, Russ

Micah 6:8

Table of contents

Damaged God for sale

Originally, I was going to title this one, "What are you advertising?" I thought it was a good title but then it seemed to me that it was too gentle for the topic. Most people would probably read the first title, start nodding and say, "Mmm hmm that's true!" We tend to expect that we already know what someone is going to say, so we decide right off the bat if we agree or not. Sadly, we usually stop listening to the writer's voice at that point. I feel this topic is too important to allow that, so I changed the title. Hang on tight!

Damaged God for sale...
God by definition is simply:

All knowing (*sees, hears, understands everything ever known or hidden, big or small*)

All powerful (*is able to do anything, big or small, no matter how impossible it seems*)

Everywhere present (*in everything, everywhere and around the entire universe all at the same time*)

Unchangeable (*unable to be changed by time or situation or any other force*) and

Eternal (*without beginning or end*)

...I said the definition was simple, I didn't say it was... easy to understand.

We have to understand that God has to be... God, or He's something else, **something less**. <u>Our God is either ALL of those things in the list or He is simply NOT GOD.</u>

God is not just "smarter than us," He's All Knowing...
                              If He's really GOD!
God is not just "stronger than us," He's All Powerful...
                              If He's really GOD!
God is not just "bigger than us," He's Everywhere Present...
                              If He's really GOD!
God is not just "better than us," He's Completely Unchangeable...
                              If He's really GOD!

...and, if God is GOD, then He keeps His word, He WILL do what He says He will do and, what He says is absolutely TRUE. Always and forever! *If God is really GOD*

So what kind of God are we selling with our lives? Are we selling a damaged God? An 80% God? A generic, refurbished God? An "off-brand" God copy? A God with MOST of the parts???

If God tells us to not fear, because He is always with us, but we live in fear and apprehension, then it's a damaged God we're trying to sell. If God tells us to love our enemies and do good to those who are mean to us, but we want revenge (*justice*) and celebrate getting even, then it's a damaged God we're trying to sell. (*YES, this is convicting and uncomfortable for me too*).

All the little things in our walks that we dismiss as "*oops, that's just me*" or "*I'm only human,*" might just be our excuses for selling a damaged God to the world around us.

Before Jesus came, the children of Israel had God's instruction book. They had all the truth they needed, to live life rightly. They even had prophets to help them and God's assurance that if they allowed Him, He would be all they needed in every situation. However, they sold a damaged God to each other and the peoples around them, by not living like God was really GOD!

WE have the example of Jesus and we have the Holy Spirit living inside us. Yet, we often live like we follow something limited in strength, something prone to failure, a nicer occasionally useful option. God isn't supposed to be something we hope works for us most of the time. He is supposed to be the one and only thing in our lives that we can always and completely count on! If people in our lives aren't amazed at the God they see us walk with, maybe we're selling a damaged God.

Peas and carrots

There are themes that repeat in our walk with God. One of these themes is patience.

James 1:2-4 *My brethren, count it all joy when ye fall into divers temptations; knowing this, that the trying of your faith worketh patience. But let patience have her perfect work, that ye may be perfect and entire, wanting nothing.*

Romans 5:3-4 *And not only so, but we glory in tribulations also: knowing that tribulation worketh patience; and patience, experience; and experience, hope:*

Even though we know this is a simple fact of faith, nobody likes to be reminded that we all could use more patience, *mostly because we all know what cost is usually attached to it.*

So, one visual that I try to keep in mind is a very long dinner table. This table is so long that you can't see the far end. Your side of the table has chairs and place settings all the way down, dozens of them, one after the other. Each setting has a covered dish in front of it.

There are only 5 things that you know for sure at this feast.
1 - Jesus is the chef of each course. He stands in front of you until you finish at that chair.
2 - Jesus tells you when you are done with each particular plate. Only He knows how much you need to eat before you can move on.
3 - Each plate has different food from the ones before.
4 - You won't know what type of food is under each dish cover, until Jesus reveals it to you.
5 - You know that your life-journey ends when you finish some undisclosed plate of food further down the table.

(Yes, my brain actually works like this, stay with me.)

11

I hope you can picture this table. It's the table of your life and you are there with Jesus alone!

Honestly, the way we usually deal with seasons in our life is kind of like this. If Jesus reveals a food (*a season*) we like, we are quite content to sit at that table and savor every bite. "Mmmm...This is so good!" Thanks Jesus... can I have some more please?" Yet, when we He reveals a food we don't like, we want to rush through it and get it over with so we can move onto the next plate... hoping it's something we "like better." *We even try to skip an unpleasant plate if we can get away with it.*

The thing with Chef Jesus is that He doesn't let you move on until <u>He decides</u> that you're finished with your peas and carrots.

You see, from His 'all-knowing' point of view, time is an opportunity for clarity in our lives. TIME IS AN OPPORTUNITY FOR CLARITY! The seasons we spend at the plate of peas and carrots are not punishment or summer school.

We have this urgency to see our time as our most valuable commodity, but God says, "NO," WE are his most valuable commodity!! See, of all the places that God lives (*in Heaven, in us, in time*), TIME is the one He will get rid of one day. It has less value than we do to Him. This plate He has before us is perfect. Yes, I want to get to the turkey, mashed potatoes and gravy plate, ...but right now, these peas and carrots are perfect!!!

Here's the key - stop looking at the food on your plate and deciding if you like it or not, don't keep glancing down the table wondering if the next plate is going to be better, ...<u>start staring at the chef who prepared it for you</u>!!!!!!!! Then, when you see the kind eyes, the desire He has to talk with you at this plate and be known by you better. You lose the desire to rush.

If He asks us to eat 3 portions of peas and carrots or just 3 bites, it won't matter because <u>we are dining with Him</u>!

Two dollar beer full of hope

I went to McDonalds one morning and while in line, I was approached by a sort of scraggly looking gentleman. He said he needed two dollars for gas to get home and asked if I could help him out? I reached into my pocket and pulled out the two dollars, sending him on his way toward the gas station across the street, as I continued to wait in line. A few minutes later, I was back in my car and on my way. As I pulled up to the traffic light between the McDonalds and the gas station, I saw the same man emerge with a can of beer and walk across the street in the opposite direction. I think you can all understand the flurry of feelings and questions I had at that moment.

"Oh c'mon God, how can you let him get away with this?"

"Am I an idiot for believing him or what?"

"Should I go and let him see that I caught him in his horrible lie?"
(...*and more like these*)

Thankfully, I couldn't deal with those questions right then, I only had a couple minutes to pick my wife up from an appointment she had, so I drove off in the other direction to get my Sweety.

God does that sometimes, forces us to pause before we head down a wrong path. As I drove to get my wife, it occurred to me that those earlier questions were probably the very ones the devil would love for me to focus on. He always tries to get us to see the unfair in everything, pointing at the wrong and making a fuss over it. *I can do that so easily and it's such a waste of energy.*

I kind of felt the Holy Spirit whisper in reaction to my questions, "*so what?*" *What are you going to do about it?"* A quietness spoke within me saying, "I will still give and hope for better." Suddenly I realized that it was his actions, his lie, that was being used by the devil to get me to say '*no*' to the next person in need. ***Unfair toward me, ...to grow unmerciful toward others?*** Oh well played devil! I thank God for those times when the Holy Spirit walks me beyond natural understanding. *This was one of those times.*

I picked up my wife and in the car I tell her what happened and that I want to go find the guy and tell him something. She seemed sure this was a bad idea. She is a lot smarter than I am. I explained that I wanted to tell him that I wasn't mad at him and most importantly, that his actions would not stop me from helping and caring. I wanted him to know that his lie wasn't stronger than the hope in me. I wanted to let him know that if he lies to people like that, it may be his fault when some good Samaritan gives up and a real little kid goes hungry.

Obviously, be smart and pray first, but, if you're reading this and you've been taken advantage of when helping others, I am sorry and no, it's not fair. Please though, please remember, when you quit, it's the next needy person that will suffer. Don't give power to someone else's lie. Guess what? Jesus got used too! Luke 17:12-19 He healed 10 lepers and only one came back to thank Him. Jesus healed out of love for others. Not to balance an equation. Not for an "if-then." Not for a show of power. Just because His heart loved so freely, that His actions followed recklessly! Let's be like that. It's so much more beautiful than giving power to the lies and tricks of others.

Don't let "unfair toward you," grow seeds of "unmerciful toward others."

A broken bride

I will begin this with one of my own personal building-block thoughts. I don't say it out loud very often but I believe it with all my heart.

"Before a man can truly be a husband, he must first learn to be a bride of Christ."

Meaning that we need to learn how to be properly loved, before we can properly love another. I sincerely mean chased by a romantic suitor, wooed and won. Jesus has pursued us relentlessly <u>to win our hearts, not just purchase our forgiveness</u>!

My friends, God's goal is not just our rescue from hell, it is a 'complete relationship-reconciliation' that He wants!

As a husband, I am to love my wife as Christ loved the church and gave Himself for it. (*Eph 5:25*)

It says nothing of manage her, control her, correct her, train her or use her. It says give yourself for her. Don't make her follow you, help her to better follow her God.

Why would this be the advice given to husbands?

Didn't God state that the family order puts man at the top? Yes, it actually does put man as head of the family. To follow the example of our Savior!

Husband: love her no matter what.

Husband: tend to her emotional bruises, even the ones she got before you.

Husband: forgive her before she needs it.

Husband: overlook her faults.

Husband: let her have as many second chances as she needs.

Husband: be patient with her.

Husband: celebrate all her victories without comparing her with anyone else.

Husband: show her in your words, actions and eyes, that your heart is all hers.

There are those that might see this kind of love as being a sucker and being taken advantage of. Being a chump and a doormat. God, though, looks upon this kind of love and says, **"NOW, I see my son in you"**.

Husband, remember, this is exactly how God treats you every moment of your life. We men, at our best, are God's broken brides.

The fact that He would trust me with one of His daughters, as my own broken bride, with the expectation that I give to her what He has given to me, is an overwhelming honor.

As I said,
Jesus has pursued us relentlessly to win our hearts, not just purchase our forgiveness!

The lame man's letter home

Several years ago, I got a part in the church Easter play. It was kind of a big deal for me. Our church went all out with lights and special effects. It brought in hundreds of people to hear the salvation message that was given at the end. This particular year, the play was based on the book of Acts. My character was the lame man from Acts 3:1-10.

"One day Peter and John were going up to the temple at the time of prayer—at three in the afternoon. Now a man who was lame from birth was being carried to the temple gate called Beautiful, where he was put every day to beg from those going into the temple courts. When he saw Peter and John about to enter, he asked them for money. Peter looked straight at him, as did John. Then Peter said, "Look at us!" So the man gave them his attention, expecting to get something from them. Then Peter said, "Silver or gold I do not have, but what I do have I give you. In the name of Jesus Christ of Nazareth, walk." Taking him by the right hand, he helped him up, and instantly the man's feet and ankles became strong. He jumped to his feet and began to walk. Then he went with them into the temple courts, walking and jumping, and praising God. When all the people saw him walking and praising God, they recognized him as the same man who used to sit begging at the temple gate called Beautiful, and they were filled with wonder and amazement at what had happened to him."

There were several performances throughout the holiday weekend and I loved the chance to be a part of it. After the last night of the play, I went home to scrape off the makeup and unwind. As I sat in the living room reflecting on the character I played, I wondered what was next for him. The Bible isn't that informative on the subject, but I am always eager to 'suppose' in the gaps, *if you know what I mean.* So, I sat down and wrote the "Lame Man's Letter " that I imagine he sent home after being healed.

Dear Mother,

I am sure you have heard the stories about what has happened to me. YES, I have been healed! My legs are whole and I can walk now. It was 2 days ago, as I sat by the same temple gate where I sat for years. A couple of men came in and I asked them for alms, as I ask every man who passes the Temple gate. But these men were different. They spoke with authority Mama, as if they were Princes, but they looked like all the other men from our street.

It happened so fast, one man named Peter, told me to look at him and that they had no money to give but that he would give what he did have. Then He spoke the name, Jesus the Christ, and told me to walk. He told me to walk! He grabbed my hand and I felt warm. I felt tingles and heat in my feet and legs, and I stood up. I didn't just stand up Mama, I jumped and ran and danced!

I am crying as I write this because I never thought I could have a life, a real life, but I am whole now. I am a man! God touched me through these men and gave me a new life. I don't know why God did this for me. My faith was dead and hope had left me but God healed me anyway. Later, the one called John told me that God had sent His son into this world to declare God's love for all of us. This Jesus was the Son of God and John said that Jesus died to forgive my sins. Never had I heard of our God being so kind before, but it must be true, for I can walk.

I know you must also be wondering why I haven't come home yet. It was my first thought, "I will go home and show my Mother what God did for me". But Mother, I had to know more. These men, they spoke of being with this Jesus, as His friends. They carry His words and even more than words, it is as if this Jesus is still with them. I have to know more, I have to know this Jesus! I will walk with them and work with them. They are fishermen. Mama, I will learn to fish! I will learn to do much and I will send you the money that I earn.

Until I come home, have faith and know that I love you. Your son, healed and loved by God.

I do not think the lame man took his healing and went back home. How could someone receive so much from God and not want to know Him more? In my mind, he MUST HAVE followed Peter and John.

Then again, have any of us received less forgiveness, less love or less hope than the lame man? I know I haven't. I too, dance and jump and run with a previously crippled heart.
Do we take these gifts and run home?
Or, do we leave our old lives behind
and follow the one who gives the gifts?

Into the out

There is a very well known verse that says, "*Behold, I stand at the door and knock.*" It can often be seen on a painting of Jesus standing outside the front door of a house waiting permission to enter. It gets used as an evangelistic tool for winning people to a loving Savior who is asking to be allowed into our hearts to forgive us. I have no problem with that at all... it's just that the verse they refer to has so much more God-stuff packed into it!

(*NIV*) Rev 3:20 says, "*Here I am! I stand at the door and knock. If anyone hears my voice and opens the door, I will come in and eat with that person, and they with me.*" So yes, Jesus is standing outside of our hearts, metaphorically speaking, knocking and patiently waiting for permission to enter. It is also true that when He enters, He brings forgiveness with Him (a*ll good stuff, right there*). But there is more to gather from this verse. So let's go back and start again.

"*Here I am*" that's Jesus, or more specifically that's my Jesus. He Himself is standing there, not a messenger or courier, but the one and only Jesus, standing at every heart on earth, knocking. How much value we must have to be approached by the Son of God Himself! How fantastic and gentle a love He must feel toward us to come and wait for our answer?

"*I stand at the door and knock*" He's not running down the street banging on a door then boom on to the next one. He is standing at the door of each heart, waiting and waiting, for the chance to begin a relationship with us. He's a gentleman, not peering in the windows or yelling, "*I know you're in there and I know what you're doing, so get out here and face me!*" He is asking us for permission, He's waiting for us to choose, He's declaring our value to Him by the way He honors our free will.

"*If anyone hears my voice and opens the door*" IF... if is a word leaving the choice up to us. It really is our decision. "*If anyone*"... because all are invited, ALL are invited by Jesus. "*If anyone hears my voice*"... the sweetest and truest sound in the universe, the voice of Jesus calling to us, "*May I come in please? I want to see you and I have something for you.*" He's at our door, it's really Him, He's here! "*Hears my voice*"... because He is speaking to all of us, our souls know that God is calling, we feel His whispers in our hearts but that's not enough. "*And opens the door*"... not just a crack with the chain still on, not open but standing in front of it blocking His way, not a single restriction of access. Opens the door means grants Him access, "welcome Lord, grab a chair".

Yes, it's scary inviting Jesus in. We fear that He's going to come in and start rearranging the furniture and throwing stuff out. We fear that he's going to start poking around in the closets and under the beds and find the stuff we hide. We fear He's going to say our hearts are filthy, turn around and walk out. We fear He's going to pull out a big list of all the things we have to give up! But He promises something far less scary.

"*I will come in and eat with that person.*" No shame, no white glove test or surprise inspection. "*I will come in*"... not a single open door will He turn away from. It doesn't matter how dirty the house is or how guilty the heart is, He will come in IF you open the door. There are no conditions to entry either. He is not going to wait for the red carpet, the accurate list of all misdeeds or even the sincere pledge to correct ever wrong and walk the straight and narrow. He wants first and foremost to come in, because <u>our forgiveness and salvation are more important to Him than our dirty past</u>.

That is the love of God toward us! "*and eat with that person*" Not have a "come-to-Jesus-meeting." Not lovingly correct you. Not sit down and let you explain yourself, but eat with you. Dinner, fellowship, conversation, a time of rest and joy. "*How was your son's soccer game today?*"

"Good Jesus, we won in overtime. Johnny even scored 2 goals!"

"I saw that, he was so excited."

"Hey Jesus, did you play sports as a kid?"

"Yes, of course I did, I also climbed trees, did chores and occasionally fell asleep in school."

"NO WAY!"

"Haha have you read the books of law and tradition?"

(*sounds wonderful right? Jesus just talking with us, having dinner with us*) *I will come in and eat with that person.* Eat with us implies (*to me*) that He will have what we are having. No special menu, just whatever we have on the stove already, Him eating with us. We do what we do and He joins us. (*obviously I am not talking about sin*) It has to do with our regular-normal-human lives, He is willing to enter into a relationship with us on those terms. He'll start there, He just wants our relationship to grow into something more. Just as He did by becoming a human baby in a dusty wilderness, He showed His desire to reach all the way into our world, become like us and lead us to His world and a better version of us. He came into our world, in order to lead us into His. (*say it again and chew it up in your heart and mind*)

- He came into our world, in order to lead us into His. -

Here comes the big point.

"...and they with me." Jesus comes into our world, has fellowship and food with us on our terms (*meaning: up to our capacity*), then He will have us eat with Him! He will prepare the meal in our house and we will eat with Him. We will sample his food, His capacity, His fellowship, His compassion and His joy. We will taste and see that the Lord is good, in Psalm 34:8. He will overwhelm us with His favor and presence. We will be left saying, "Lord this is too much and too good!" We will become aware of His capacity and the new terms that He is hoping to relate to us on, how deeply He wants to be known by us and how far from where we

currently are He wants to walk us. Our tummies will be full, our hearts and minds and hands will be full and we will want to share it. All of a sudden, this home we used to hide in becomes a place we want to share. The door we were reluctant to crack open is left unlocked and a welcome mat is placed in front of it. We may even be brave enough to ask Jesus, "Jesus, this is so much. Do you think we could take some to my neighbor? They seem like they could use some of this? They're just down the street Lord. We could pop by and give them some." *And the fulfillment of the great commission begins.* No training, no school, no degree or title, just **too much love to keep to ourselves**.

Jesus waits for us to invite Him into our lives, then, He invites us into the out! The out is His enormous life outside of our selves, outside of our comfort zone and natural abilities, outside of our financial means and retirement planning, outside of our social circles, outside of our schedules and plans, outside of everything us. Beyond our fears and past our dreams, into the out, where only He can sustain us, provide for us and lead us. This gentle knock and invitation to dinner is really the lover of our souls inviting us to know Him better and be swept away in a love strong enough to save the whole world.

Dime sized hole

Sometimes when we want to give something nice to someone else, (*which is a good thing, obviously*). We find out that they don't want it. It can be such a frustrating thing at times and we may even be deeply hurt by it. "*I want to give you something good, something much better than what you already have and you say, NO!*" That doesn't even make sense? *It can feel like, since our best gift is rejected, we have no value to that person either.*

In this case, I am talking about giving someone your time or advice, and not a money gift. Odds are that most money gifts and presents will be accepted unless the person has a special situation that keeps them from allowing you to bless them. (*perhaps an agreement with God or another person, to rely on a specific provision*)

Imagine you are talking to a friend who could use some extra wisdom for a situation they are in. They have had trouble making decisions in an area of their life and you start to share something personal from your past to encourage them to do the right thing. You aren't preaching at them, you're SHARING WITH THEM. About 3 sentences into what you are sharing, you can see in their face that they have stopped listening. That can hurt because you were being vulnerable and open to help them and you got a "*Naaaaww, I'm good.*" If this has happened to you, then you understand the frustration and the hurt of having someone that you care about reject your sincere help. *I'm sorry for that*, the problem isn't you.

Let's take this to a simple illustration. Picture a kid holding a box. It has a slot cut into the top of it. The slot is to allow other people to put change into it so this poor hungry kid can eat. The slot is the size of a dime. You see this kid on the street and your heart is moved to give her your change. You walk over to her and pull several quarters out of your pocket. You try to give them to her to help her situation and she says no because they are too big for the slot. You say,

24

"*just put them in your pocket, they can help you.*" She refuses and gives you a disappointed look for not giving her any dimes at all. A weird illustration I know, but we often do that to the Lord.

God offers us His best, His fullness, Himself and we say, "*No thank you, I'm good like this.*"
I need you to read that one more time...

God offers us His best, His fullness, Himself and we say, "*No thank you, I'm good like this.*"

Ok, just one more...

God offers us **His best**, **His fullness**, **Himself** and we say, ***No*** *thank you,* ***I'm good like this.***"

There is supposed to be a hunger for more of God and not a hunger for more ease. More change, not more comfort; more power, not more settling; more Jesus, not more you and me!
(*Jn 3:30*)

It is heartbreaking enough to be rejected when you honestly want to help, I can't imagine the pain in God's heart, offering His all to us and we fight Him tooth and nail to limit what we receive. He literally has what we need, the power, the healing, the wisdom, the peace, the comfort, the blessings, the provisions and the love, all in hands extended with a note saying I bought this for YOU, please take it. We look Him in the face and say, "No thanks, I'm good. Keep your great riches, I'm waiting for a dime!"

Will we be embarrassed in heaven when we see all He had in store for us on earth that we refused, and in doing so, denied the light it would have given the world around us???

Let's not take that chance. Just receive.

And I will be changed!

In Jeremiah 17:14, it says, "Heal me, Lord, and I will be healed; save me and I will be saved, for you are the one I praise."

Today I spent some time with a couple friends. They are older and the husband has let me know on several occasions that he is the way he is and has no intention of changing, both as a person and in his walk with God. "God accepts me the way I am, He made me this way." Certainly he has that right, as do we all, to stand our ground against change, but we often hold on to this right at a very great cost! *None of this is to say there is anything wrong with the guy, he is just the catalyst in this train of thought.*

My train of thought as I was driving away...
"Change... we have to change to grow, to be better."
"Change... if we change, we can have deeper relationships."
"Change... God won't force it upon us."
"Change... can bring healing."
(*pause*).

What was that verse? Heal me and I will be healed? What if I just replace a word or two? *I know that is not sound Biblical studying, but bear with me please.*"
Change me, Lord, and I will be changed."
"What is healing if not change? A change for the better! <u>CHANGE me, Lord, and I will be... HEALED</u>?" (*OK, THAT STOPPED ME IN MY TRACKS*).

Change me, Lord, and I will be healed. So, what if God's heart of mercy toward us is full of intention to heal, not correct? <u>What if all the change that He wants to bring into our lives, is purely to heal us?</u> What if one change is about getting us away from poisonous people or situations? What if another change is God quarantining us for some therapy to fix an emotional issue? What if God placing us in some situation, in an unfamiliar place or with new responsibilities or old friends, is not to deal with our maturity issue, but in fact, to deal with an issue blocking us from greater healing?

What if all God-prompted change, is meant to heal us *from something*?

Read it out loud again: What if all God-prompted change is meant to heal us *from something*?

 Can we picture God less like a teacher trying to improve classroom results and more like a kind physician, focused solely on our well being. Unwilling to leave our bedside until we are changed, until we are finally...well.

May our view of God be adjusted, so we continually offer ourselves up for change.

Be a pickle

I used this illustration once, to explain what Salvation is, and what it's supposed to <u>produce in us</u>. You see, meeting Jesus isn't supposed to just make us better, it is supposed to change everything on a radical level!

Back to the pickle...

A <u>cucumber</u> is a fruit. It's green, oblong, has seeds inside, it's watery and has a crunchy/bumpy skin.

A <u>pickle</u> is a (*former*) cucumber, preserved in vinegar or brine. Preserved, changed inside and out to prevent decay. (*seriously? this former cucumber won't rot in a few days, it's preserved... it has a new ending to it's story*)

Here's the point. We are supposed to be changed. Look, I know and God knows, it won't all happen overnight. But whatever is happening to you should be a profound change. Your hopes and dreams refocused? Your choices of entertainment realigned? Those things demanding your attention reprioritized?

Is this process scary? Yes at times, you may feel like your losing yourself, but really, you're just losing those things that you were told, you were. (*told by everyone but God*) Jesus, like a great sculptor, just wants to get rid of the pieces that get in the way of seeing the masterpiece underneath. The rubble, the fleshly, selfish bits of 'stone' He needs to get rid of to reveal the best version of you!

The funny thing about the whole cucumber to pickle transformation is that it can't be reversed by anything ever.

<u>It's permanent</u>!

In the same way, God doesn't want us to be better cucumbers, better people... **'nicer-us' isn't the goal**. We are supposed to be <u>changed</u>. Plugged into an entirely different source and unable to be what we were before Jesus got to us.

UNABLE TO BE WHAT WE WERE BEFORE JESUS! John 10:10 "I have come that they may have life, and have it to the full." (*Zoe life, abundant life, transformed and preserving life*)

Be changed, be transformed, be... a pickle, unable to be what you were before!

Concerning fear

I just watched a video posted by a friend. It was a compilation of abandoned dog rescues. One of the dogs was a puppy who was too frightened to lay down or run or submit to the rescuer. His tail was between his legs and his rump was on the ground. He wouldn't make eye contact just drag himself in circles.

Too scared to run and too scared to stay!!! In other words, ...<u>without hope</u>. It was heartbreaking to think that this pup felt there was <u>no possibility of a good outcome</u> and it could only beg for a mercifully speedy end.

FEAR'S final goal is a complete inability to receive or accept true love. The plan of evil is to keep us at arms length from God, from salvation, from healing, from peace, from fulfilling our destiny.

Fear was never meant to be a part of creation. The Garden was perfect, then <u>sin ushered in fear</u>. The very first child born, murdered his little brother and mankind has courted evil ever since.

What has fear done to you? What corner has it backed you into? What lie has it convinced you to hold onto with both hands?

How many of us have been too scared to run and too scared to stay, <u>at one time in our lives</u>? How many people live with that as their normal??? I believe we are in a world of "too scared," a world desperately in need of some hope.

Fear is a masterful lie from the devil who rejected God's love. Satan lives to get us to reject God's love as well. Knowing full well that we are made to reside in God's perfect love and that "perfect love casts out fear *(1 Jn 4:18)*. " **Our fear is the devil's delight!** Makes you sort of sick seeing it that way huh? Me too.

Hope is a weapon against fear. *HOPE: the anticipation of something happening based on a feeling of trust.* The love of God is so pure and strong that, the hope which springs from it, gets us to lay down the facts of a fearful situation and cling to a God we can't see. 'Hope maketh not ashamed' in Rom 5:5-8 (*well worth reading.*) Hope is intended to be a tether that reaches over fear and connects us to God's love.

I'm sure the puppy, once rescued and loved on a consistent basis, learned to have hope. Hope that it's new owner would return from work each day. Hope that the bowl would be full of food each day and hope that the neglect and pain are over. I'm also sure that this hope led to the puppy growing to accept a relationship of love.

We all need hope.

If you have hope, please don't keep it to yourself, share it. It's more valuable than diamonds and gold! Share your Jesus. Share what He's blessed you with. Share your expectations based on trusting God. In the end, we know that fear will be stripped powerless and cast into the furnace by Jesus. And hope will be realized, the expectation manifested. All fear will be forgotten in the embrace of perfect love!

The very same perfect love that already showed up on a wooden cross. So we don't have to wait, let's get lost in His embrace now.

Afraid of generosity

Quite often we tell ourselves that we would be more generous if we just had some more. More money, more time, more food, more energy, more, more, more... It seems to be our most used excuse about why we don't give or help.

Don't get me wrong here. I'm not calling anyone selfish. My hope is that we get free of fear's hold in this area. Generosity has very little to do with our bank accounts and everything to do with our 'Thank-accounts." *Once again*:

Generosity has very little to do with our bank accounts and everything to do with our 'Thank-accounts'!

Often we are asked to be generous with our time or money, sometimes we are strongly encouraged or even guilted into being generous... for a "worthy cause". What happens in that moment is someone directs our focus, to a need. Usually it's an undeniable need with an emotional struggle. We are focused on this need then handed a responsibility for it, "If you don't help, the kids won't eat!" Then usually, our focus is directed to our own surplus, "Couldn't you spare just a dollar a day?" It's this surprise equation thrust upon us, that we hate because we have to answer it with either a "Yes I can give you a dollar a day so the kids don't die of starvation" or a "Nope, it's my money and I'm keeping it. I earned it and I have plans for it." This gives us a choice, either we admit to being selfish and let the hungry kids die or allow ourselves to be robbed in front of everyone and then thank them for it. I'm serious! Where God plans for us to be cheerful voluntary givers, the devil seeks to take the joy out of sacrifice and leaves us with guilt, shame, obligation and a strong desire to avoid all other pleas for help.

Children are so good at being cheerful voluntary givers. "Hey do you want part of my donut? I have a PB&J, you can have it if you want! Wanna try my bike?" Giving is supposed to be the simple act of sharing. Sharing from a

31

content heart, from an unnamed childhood condition called 'thankfulness'. I remember watching my young son be generous with everything. His words and time, his hands and strength, his stuff and ...my money. Is that the key right there? Him just expecting that his Dad was good too and *I would back him up with my wallet each time he decided to do what's right and decent?*

What if we stopped looking at the stuff that we have, as some commodity the we gathered all by ourselves and need to hide under the bed? Could we find the freedom to trust our Dad to replace whatever we give away <u>in His name</u>? Perhaps we are never really emptying our own storehouse. Perhaps we are never really giving away from our own supply. What if all of our treasures here on earth, are just "the goods" He has asked us to deliver to others?

What if we only have stuff here on earth because God needs us to share it or deliver it to others? I guess that would be asking too much of us if He didn't already have OUR REWARD, <u>our stuff to have</u>, waiting for us when we get home (*Heaven*)!

We all have to look in the mirror and ask ourselves, "Should my generosity be solely based on whether or not I believe His nature and His promises?"

THAT is a good question -

When God says, "I don't care."

(my reasons why I'm not worthy)

I know I'm not the only one who does that. I often give God my list of why He shouldn't choose me. Why I'm the worst choice and ANYONE else would be better. I even suggest other names sometimes. "Lord, you should get *this guy* to do it!" I may not actually say it out loud, but I secretly disqualify myself from the very 'abundant life' that God has invited me to. In John 10:10 it says, "*The thief does not come except to steal, and to kill, and to destroy. I have come that they may have life, and that they may have it more abundantly.*"

That is Jesus talking there, not some guy named Sean who sells used boots or something. Jesus, the living Son of God, nothing but truth comes from His mouth and He says, "I have come that they may have life, and that they may have it more abundantly." He also says in John 14:12, that we will do greater things than He did. Seriously? What's the catch?

The catch is in the word **'may'**. We may have an abundant life (*and do greater things as part of it*), if we allow God that kind of access to us, if we don't disqualify ourselves and back away from what He has invited us to be a part of. We have to picture God saying, "yea so? I don't care, I already knew that before I invited you", to all of our excuses. (*let's just try that*)

Picture God as a very excited Dad wanting to spend time with us and prove to us that He believes in us more than we do. We are sitting across the breakfast table from Him. He puts down the paper and pushes His bowl of Captain Crunch aside. He's leaning in toward us longing for eye contact as He offers us the adventure He's been planning to share!

"Hey guess what I'm doing today? I'd love your help with it!"

"Gee Dad, I'm terrible at that." *"Yea so? I don't care, I already knew that before I invited you."*

"Uhm, Susan is better at that than I am." *"Yea so? I don't care, I already knew that before I invited you."*

"I'm too scared to try that.'" *"Yea so? I don't care, I already knew that before I invited you."*

"You know I don't have any background in that right?" *"Yea so? I don't care, I already knew that before I invited you."*

"That sounds impossible." *"Yea so? I don't care, I already knew that before I invited you."*

(*...or the more grown up versions...*)

"I... well, honestly, I don't deserve to go.' *"Yea so? I don't care, I already knew that before I invited you."*

"But I have messed up so many other things." *"Yea so? I don't care, I already knew that before I invited you."*

"Don't you remember how I was just so rotten to you?" *"Yea so? I don't care, I already knew that before I invited you."*

"I can't, I have to be responsible and act like an adult." *Yea so? I don't care, I already knew that before I invited you."*

I think if we picture an actual conversation with God like that, it's easier to realize His goal is more about spending time <u>with us</u> and helping us reach for the best version ourselves, than 'getting the job done'.

So what is our excuse, our reason to say no to God? Honestly, I think God just hears 'NO' when we give him excuses. Can we picture the very Savior who died for us, standing in front of us as we say, "No, I don't want to spend time with you"? How Peter's heart must have broken at all his excuses for denying Jesus the day he was taken. He was scared. He was worried. He had every right to say, "I don't know Him".

Sadly, that was the truth. Peter didn't know Him in a way where he could just say yes to the scary, yes to the impossible and yes to the unknown, because it would all be WITH JESUS. But years later, oh this frightened Peter just wanted to be with his best friend Jesus and stopped making excuses. That's when Peter started to change the entire world! *Which was the simple invitation that Jesus originally offered him anyway.*

I don't know why He decided to see us the way He does, with so much love and hope and a belief that we are worth His own life. I only know that if He's inviting me to do something with Him, I want... to want, ...to say YES!

Is this faith? Yes, but it's also the amazing storm we call LOVE!

Double meat please!

There is a sandwich store that advertises the option of getting twice the meat on your sandwich. You just have to say "Double Meat," when ordering it.

Here's another odd way of reaching a simple spiritual conclusion.

My wife and I were talking about ways to avoid discontentment with churches. We have had several friends in the past that have left the churches they were attending. Leaving your church isn't always a bad thing. Sometimes, it's just time to move on, sometimes it's important to take a stand for Holiness and love, sometime's God just wants to break up things before they get weird. There are instances though, when the flesh and the devil stir up feelings of discontentment that are directly connected to lies. I have heard one lie, a lot more than others, "I'm not getting any meat at this church." *Meaning: the teaching here isn't Bible-y enough for me, this is milk or spiritual baby-food.*
This phrase comes from 1 Cor 3:2 where Paul is telling some people that they are immature and like a young child, they need to have milk (*simple lessons*) for food. He says they are not spiritually mature enough to feed on the meat (*deeper lessons*) of God's Word. Many in churches have come to think that learning the Hebrew and Greek of the Bible or learning all about the historical settings, is that 'meat' that Paul was speaking about. The problem with calling Biblical education "meat," is that we place the emphasis on knowledge. Did we see the geniuses that Jesus picked to be His 12 followers? A group made up mostly of common fisherman who got in arguments. So maybe MEAT is really something else?
When someone leaves a church looking for more meat, sometimes they are saying, "I want to be taught more information" or "I want more explanations for the things regular people don't know." *I apologize if this seems harsh,*

that is not my intention, but there is a point we need to follow this to.

It's as if John 3:16 couldn't be enough to transform the world. These people want to stay in religious school so they can gather enough knowledge to make a difference. I think most of these people are honestly trying to do the right thing! "*GIVE me more of God, so I can then be ready to do what He asks!*" - Double meat please!!!

Here's where I think the meat issue gets a bit confused. In John 4:34, Jesus tells His friends that 'doing God's will' is His meat. DOING GOD'S WILL was meat to Jesus, not more knowledge, lectures or information. It was as if Jesus was taking the whole "*give me more of God, so I can then be ready to do what He asks*" thing and flipping it around. Could Jesus be saying that "*doing what God asks, is exactly how you get more of God*"?

"Doing what God asks is how you get more of God!"

Well, that changes everything. In human-life, we gather enough for ourselves THEN we might have a bit more to give away. In God-life, we give away to make room for God to give more! Look at the life of Jesus, which one sounds more like Him? Do we honestly think Jesus came to live an example that we aren't supposed to follow?

Asking for more, before we can start doing, is a very sticky trap. We may find ourselves years into a process of gathering, but still unwilling to give or do. I have been given so much already, that I could spend my entire life serving and never repay God. *What about you*?

Those fishermen knew they were loved and forgiven by God. The religious leaders who tried to stop them knew the Hebrew and all the traditions. One group claimed to have the meat... one group just lived it.

Which ones changed the world?

Every weight

"...let us lay aside <u>every weight</u>, and the sin which doth so easily besets us, ..." Heb 12:1

So, I don't usually just start out with a bible verse, but in this case, it's the right way to begin our conversation. I heard a wonderful sermon the other day on this subject and the Pastor focused on the idea of the weights in this verse. He said the sins issue is what normally gets mentioned but he felt that he wanted to look a bit more at the 'weights' God speaks of here.

In his message, he spoke of **fears** as weights, which I agree with completely, but my brain drifted down a slightly different path. <u>The good things that get in the way of God things</u>! Careers, family, dreams, good causes, being right, ...all things that don't seem bad at all, but quite honestly, <u>they have the ability</u> to slip right between us and God with very little effort.

Weights don't have to start out as sins. Look at most religions. They usually come from someone trying to figure out the best way to connect to God. That's good. Then something gets a bit confused and they make the religion into their god! From there they start mistreating those who disagree with them or worse. That's sin. What started out as a desire for good, a desire for God, became an evil weight and a huge sin.

This follows the devil's favorite plan for tricking us, the "subtle counterfeit."

How victorious for Satan if he can get us to turn the blessings of God into <u>the very things that come between God and us</u>. God's blessings turned to "weights." Turned to sins! It can happen any minute of any day. We can lose to convenience, we can lose to happiness and we can lose to love. What could really 'beset us' as easily as something we like or love or want and that feels like a blessing?

So what's the plan to safeguard our selves from this trap? How do we keep the things of God from coming between Him and us?

This brought the Old Testament into a better light for me. See, God had given His kids some great suggestions for habits to encourage a proper perspective between the gifts and the **gift-giver**. He had them set up pillars of rocks to remind them every time they passed by, of the victory or miracle that happened there. They put a prayer on the doorway that entered their homes to remind them of God's personal intervention in their individual lives. He had them establish traditions and feasts to remind them of a season of deliverance in their stories.

Maybe it's the lack of personal celebration of God's moving in our own stories that makes it so easy to forget? Maybe that is the whole reason for *Phi 4:8* "thinking on these things"? We are such creatures of habit that we need to make "Gratitude toward God" a purposed habit or apathy will surely grow in its place. Talk to God, glean from others and make your reminders wonderful! Reliving our faith, sharing our experiences, revealing your God... it's a flag that needs to be hoisted every day because, though the gifts of God are great indeed, they are not God and shouldn't become weights between Him and us.

When **anything** gets in the way of "God and us," they become weights.

The tweezers come out

I picture it like this; we are a vessel, a huge vessel, ready to be filled. The problem is that there are a few choices for what fills us. Obviously, God wants to fill us with His wisdom, love, power and it would be the best thing for us to allow and even invite in. There is the devil who hates us completely and wants to fill us with doubt, pain and distraction. Lastly (*and I am over-simplifying*) there is us, (*ourselves*) with our dreams, fears, problems, cultural influences, family influences, friends and media influences. That is a lot of stuff that pushes for access into our sense of self. Wait! ...oh and I almost forgot, there is this oily goo called sin that bubbles up from inside our base, infecting almost everything else that we put into our vessel. Like an uncapped permanent marker, staining everything else that gets thrown into the laundry basket. It seeps and spreads and ruins everything!

We get the idea of sin it's bad right? It's disobeying God and if you let it, it will make you do really bad things. Those who give in all the way become murderers and junk like that. The best thing to do is follow all the religious rules and you'll be fine. **NO, that's not right!**

Sin is poison and it comes from within and <u>we don't have a cure</u>. It poisons and poisons and poisons... let's remember that it's so powerful that only the blood of Jesus could break the power it had over our eternal destination. *It would be worthy of fearing, if not for the Grace of God, which is more powerful.* We always have this hidden spring of evil inside us, no matter who we are and how well we're doing. The funny thing is that we often subconsciously think that once we get saved and start really following God, that the sin within us is sort of a minor, almost gone, kind of issue. However, it's still just as strong, just as evil, but now we are adding the things of God to water it down. More good in our vessel fighting the sin in our vessel. There's an old saying, G.I.G.O. (*garbage in, garbage out*) meaning that we can only get out of ourselves, the things that we put into ourselves. If

I fill a bag (*or my vessel*) with only banana peels and apple cores, then I will never be able to pull a strawberry milkshake out of the bag (*or a kind word from my vessel*).

Where do the tweezers come in? Let me shift the analogy a bit from uncapped markers and gooey springs of poison, to a vessel partially filled with poppy seeds. Those tiny little black seeds on some bagels that get stuck in your teeth and it seems like you can never pick or brush them all out. So sin is poppy seeds in our vessel and the God stuff is uncooked rice. Picturing it with me? Now our vessel leaks, it's a side effect of being broken by sin, there are cracks and holes, so the good stuff leaks out. So we can picture the rice running out of the sides but the tiny poppy seeds settle down between them and stay in the vessel. THAT is sin. Sin doesn't go away even though it's fully paid for by the cross. It doesn't go away... until we finish this life. Somewhere between our last breath and our entrance into heaven, God pulls out the tweezers and pulls every single tiny seed of poisonous sin from us. That gooey spring is sealed up, removed and cast away. Me without sin... US without sin, only happens in heaven.

We must, <u>absolutely must</u>, keep in mind that we are all still dealing with sin until then. ALL OF US, nobody is excluded, not a single person is free from the influence of sin. Those who belong to Jesus are free from the eternal consequences, but not from the influence of sin. This is to keep us humble and aware of the overwhelming need to be kind, understanding and compassionate to everyone.

We don't have to allow evil or sin, but we should be understanding of those trapped in it, because the tweezers only come out on the way to heaven!

FREE refills

I once posted online...
"Jesus invented FREE REFILLS!"
It came after thinking about how often He is willing to pick me up, dust me off and fill me again with his spirit and love. The unending 2nd chances, the limitless access to the throne of Grace and Mercy. The cup of forgiveness that never runs dry. <u>Free refills</u>!

You would think that a God of free refills would have a longer line at the door. People waiting for the chance to come in and get refilled, forgiven, rekindled, redirected, and encouraged again, all for free. That's what I would expect in a world so full of messed up decisions, regret and shame, people lined up for <u>the God of free refills</u>! "Do-over's" just being handed out to everyone in need of one, all paid for and ready to go. So why isn't there a line for this God?

Maybe it's us.

Surely those who follow a God of free refills are advertising Him correctly right? That's the big sign we should all be carrying, instead of pointing fingers and yelling, "You're empty!"

There was this lady who was caught doing bad stuff, the Bible calls her the woman 'taken in adultery'. John 8 tells the story of how all the people who saw her, pointed and said, "You're empty (*of righteousness, empty of anything worth loving, empty of value*)." Ok that wasn't their words but it was their meaning and they were going to kill her for being empty, because they thought of themselves as full. Then Jesus spoke to her and invited her to be refilled! The people of the town had pointed and called her empty, but Jesus knew that God has free refills for the thirsty, the empty, the leaking. We are like jars with cracks in them and if we don't stay close to the source of refills, we run empty and dry up. If we look at the life and words of Jesus, He spent every moment advertising the God of FREE refills.

So what about us? Maybe, just maybe, if we lived like Jesus gives US free refills, the thirsty around us will get in line for them selves too.

Are **you** feeling a bit empty today? Are you dry and feeling nothing? Are you sunk into a place without a single drop of joy? Push your way up to the counter, look right at Jesus with your heart held out toward Him and say, "**Can I get a refill please?**"

You know the old folks that work at Chik-fil-a? They just walk around looking at the tables where people are sitting and eating. They are looking, watching and paying detailed attention to who is running low. Then they come up very kindly and ask you if you'd like them to get you a refill of your drink. Isn't that exactly how Jesus lived and asks us to live? Look at people, see them and listen to them. See if they act empty then kindly and very sincerely tell them that you can show them where to get FREE refills. Jesus is always waiting at the counter with a smile!

Get off the bus, Russ

(Warning: *adult situation ahead*)   *This is a personal experience that made a profound impact on me and changed the way I saw religion, love, guilt and shame!*

I was attending a Bible college in my younger days. I was very happy there, learning doctrine and clean living, serving and reaching the lost. We were taught a lot of truth from God's Word! I was part of the clown ministry and was invited to go to New York City during Christmas break to do some evangelizing. I was excited, what an honor to be invited to share the good news with the lost of NYC. We rode down in a bus and parked it outside an affiliated church. Each buss had a couple of young men as leaders. These were strong, seasoned Bible College Students, full of zeal for God. We got off the bus and walked a few blocks to a large area where we spent the next several hours doing mimes, songs, skits and handing out religious tracts (*all very normal things for our Bible College*).

After 4 or 5 hours of this joyous ministry to the peoples of New York, we headed back to the bus. We boarded and waited for the leaders to finish paperwork, close the door, pray and guide us safely home. As we waited, most of us on the bus were sharing our favorite encounters from the day, with our nearest seatmates. It was only about 5 minutes later when one of the bus riders noticed a young lady who walked into our section of the street. She was walking slowly and asking questions of the men who walked past her. One of the ladies on the bus yelled out, "She's a hooker!" Another yelled, "that's disgusting, how dare she, right in front of the church!"

I have to admit, I wasn't sure how I was feeling, it all happened so fast. The next thing I know, the bus leaders said, "we'll see about that!" They popped open the doors and walked quickly over to the young lady to confront her. I couldn't hear the conversations but I saw the guys from the bus point fingers at her and begin to speak with authority. She stood there and listened. From inside the bus there were a lot of "that's right" and "she won't be doing that here anymore!" My head was spinning a bit, it all happened so fast.

The very next thing I saw was the young lady, desperately in need of hope and unconditional love, burst into tears and run away. The cheers on the bus made my stomach upset! The guys returned to applause, but all I heard was a quiet whisper in my heart, "that wasn't my heart for her." I knew it wasn't what my Jesus would do. I heard a tug, "get off the bus and hug her and tell her... I'm sorry." I froze! My religious brain told me that the leaders knew best and I can't miss the bus, they're ready to leave now! (*my heart knew better than that*)

I just sat on the bus and cried all the way home. I know the pain of the shame that I was feeling probably was nothing compared to the shame inflicted upon the young lady by *"God's people."* <u>I was a coward</u>. I was a Pharisee, an enemy of God and a destroyer of those He came to love. My religion failed the test!

It was a simple whisper, *"get off the bus, Russ,"* but I heeded the religious crowd and not the Spirit of God. It still haunts me. It haunts me as a vivid reminder of the difference between religion and God, and the opposing powers they wield. Condemnation or Restoration? I relive it often, on purpose. May I never forget what damage a religious mob can cause. It reminds me that **a sinner is already a prisoner, why would I want to add to their chains?**

I often pray for her and ask God to make His kindness known to her.

So, that's my personal story. I carry it as a measure of God's patience in teaching me His ways and His heart! John 8:7 *"...He that is without sin among you, let him first cast a stone at her."*

I was not, and never will be, a sinless man!

How about you?

Caught not taught

It has been said that for children, "Faith is caught, not taught." Meaning that they learn more from our example than from our instructions. *Honestly, I believe that's true for all of us.*

I guess as we reflect upon Bible times, we see this as well. The Old Testament was full of instruction and had a couple good examples of living by faith, but it seems like most folks back then just couldn't figure out how to do what God wanted them to do. There was a sort of disconnect between what God was saying and what He meant. So people came up with a lot of religious stuff that seemed easier to them. These people spent less time living their own lives the right way and more time telling everyone else what they were doing wrong.

Then, Jesus shows up and people meet Him. They get to see exactly what God was talking about. Even better, Jesus showed them that He was living out an example of what God had instructed. He lived connected to God. Some who saw Jesus said in their hearts, "oh finally, we get it," and they were changed forever! They followed Him and followed His example.

I guess the question is why? Why did seeing His faith, change theirs? Every time He said 'love your neighbor' and then He fed them, they saw how it worked. It became more real, more honest. Every time he said 'God loves you' and then He forgave someone's sins, it got more real. When they saw Him live out lesson after lesson, instruction after instruction, His Heavenly Father became more and more real. Jesus showed that his actions matched His faith.
He wasn't speaking rules for us to live by and then not doing them Himself. His actions proved that His words were true!
His actions proved that His words were true!!!
So that's our standard to live by. *No, seriously, we are told by God to live as Jesus did*! Jesus came to show us how to live a faith that is worth catching. That is why after more than 2000 years, people are still following Jesus. He proved His

words were true, by His actions. He declared God's love and lived it toward all he met. He declared God's forgiveness and offered it to all that came to Him, even those who were mean and rotten.

Can we say that we do that?

He declared God's strength and truth and patience and hope. He lived them all toward each person in His story. Those that walked with Him caught His faith and met the "Great I Am" in it. Their lives were changed and they did the impossible. The faith they caught carried them all the days of their lives because it was real and alive, not just a Sunday-school instruction.

May we never give less to the people that God entrusts to us, *especially the kids.* They face many challenges, some from within and some from the world around them. They don't need to be taught more rules. They need an example of love, truth, mercy, goodness, patience, hope and faith that they can catch.   *(Don't we all?)*

So I have to ask you,

"Do YOUR actions prove to others, that your FAITH is real?"

A pen without ink

I've always liked pens. I love drawing in pen and ink. I have favorite pens for writing and doodling and drawing. I usually lose my pens before they are used up, but once in a while I am able to hang on to one until there is no more ink in it.

I asked my Sweety what she thought of the phrase, "a pen without ink".

Her quick answer was, "Useless!"

I smiled because she gave me the answer I hoped for.

<u>Was it useless or fully-used</u>?

The outside is scratched, worn, and unrecognizable. The inside is empty, spent and completely used up. I want to look like this when I reach heaven.

Please Lord, use all of me up here!!!

A lot of my understanding has changed over time. The picture of entering the pearly gates dressed in a white robe, teeth shining, a sparkle in my eye and a perfect report card in hand... has died. I know that my report card for this life will be given to me by my Savior, with my grades replaced by His own, so I don't have any delusion of being able to offer Him anything but myself.

May I instead, offer Him a spent and fully used me.

Jesus' life is the example of the best offering we can give to God. Be used up, poured out, spent... for love, for the Gospel, for mercy, for grace, for salvations, for kindness, for friends and strangers, for Jesus.

The empty pen that I keep on my desk is a special reminder and my deepest hope. Every drop of ink that was put in that pen was used. It's not sitting half full in a drawer or almost empty in the trash. It is in the presence of its owner, completely used for the purpose it was made and purchased! Could there be a happier, more fulfilled pen?

Could there be a pen more thrilled with its journey? Could there be a pen more ready to fall into its eternal rest with a glad heart? Could there be a pen with less regret and guilt? Could there be a more thankful, contented pen than a pen without ink?

That is my goal -
May I return to my God as an empty pen.

Demanding justice

People frequently gather together around a cause and start raising their unified voices...

...in A CALL FOR JUSTICE!"

Often we're told there's a need for some social change, when in fact, what people usually really want is an act of retribution, revenge or reparation and a declaration that 'we' are right and 'they' are wrong.

"Fix this one thing **the way I want it fixed** and we'll call it justice."

The thing with justice is this, justice doesn't make up the rules, it merely upholds the already established rules and it does so without any regard for excuses. Nobody has any advantage with justice; guilty is guilty, end of story.

Synonyms for justice are: *fairness,* ***impartiality, objectivity, neutrality and honesty***

Usually the public is only interested in it's own version of <u>fairness</u>, what the crowd thinks would be fair, and it has very little interest in impartiality, objectivity and neutrality! (*for impartiality can't be bought or influenced by crowds, t-shirts or tears*)

Here is the truth! 'Justice' is a very large clawed creature that hears no excuses and accepts no deferred payments. Justice has a job that allows no special treatment, no favors and no looking the other way. If Justice is ever loosed on this planet, there will be only lifeless bodies everywhere. Justice says hurting others is wrong, justice says taking what's not yours is wrong, justice says only the giver determines what's free, not the asker, justice says lies are wrong, lust is wrong, greed is wrong, all addictions are wrong, gluttony is wrong, ignoring the needs of strangers is wrong, anger is wrong and hatred is wrong.

Not one of us would be standing, if Justice were released.

Justice carries no yardstick to compare what or who is most wrong. It just declares that wrong is wrong! This is why Justice is often pictured as a blindfolded woman holding a scale in one hand and a sword in the other.

The problem with this picture now, is that we have changed what's on the scales she holds. What we picture on the scales is US on one side and THEM on the other. (*whoever your THEM is*) What's supposed to be there is simply ME on one side and the LAW on the other. The law of God!

ME -vs- The LAW OF GOD....... ouch! Uhhm Lord, please help me in the face of justice or I won't make it and then she will bring the sword!

Mercy is what we need to release, not justice. MERCY kisses the sour face of judgment (*on the cross*) and pays the price for us all. MERCY brings life where there is pain... Justice just spreads the pain around!!!!!!!! Mercy restores balance to the scale. Mercy is freedom, freedom from judgment!

We all need to ask ourselves, am I so arrogant as to demand someone else face the scales that I was rescued from? Mercy is the fix for social injustice. Mercy is what needs to be spread like a blanket over mankind. Mercy is the only cord that can connect us all! Justice condemns all, mercy liberates all.

"A CALL FOR MERCY!!!!" that was Jesus' idea, let's go with that - Hugs

HAHA contracts

There are things in life I don't know much about or don't understand at all. These things could give me great anxiety, because we humans hate the unknown. So when things get a bit '*iffy*' for me, I choose to think instead on the things I do know, and build my hopes on them. One of these scenarios is what I lovingly call, the '*HAHA CONTRACT*'.

I do not claim to know all the 'ins and outs of salvation'. Now, I don't mean salvation in the sense of all the eternal implications of what happens when you get saved. I am talking about the simple getting saved bit. "*Yes, Jesus I want you to forgive me and come into my life. Thank you for dying for my sins, please be my Savior.*" A lot of religious and non-religious folks believe they can determine if someone is really saved or not, by looking at their lives, their '*fruit*'.

Clearly the Bible does point to the idea of transformation and new life, in connection with salvation. There is the issue of the fruit of the spirit, which means, God grows different things in us when we are really His. If those things don't grow, then we might assume that the plant (*salvation*), must not be there at all. Continuing in sin is taken by some, as a sign that salvation is missing, even if the person has prayed or made a statement of faith. I understand these views and I am not saying they are wrong or right. I am just saying that the Jesus I have seen and known, is ridiculously generous.

He healed ten lepers though only one came back and said thank you. The other nine got to keep their healing without ever producing any fruit that we know of. My favorite example of Jesus' boundless mercy is found in the story of His own death. Jesus went to the cross. He went willingly. He bore our sins upon Himself and surrendered His life out of love. While all this is forefront in His mind, He did something else wonderful. **He made and kept an appointment!**

Could Jesus have died for our sins on a Tuesday? What about the third Thursday of the month after? Well, yes He could have. Let's be honest, Jesus could have finished His painful journey the week before! *"Boom... world saved, job done, I'm outta here!"*

Here's where Jesus overwhelms me. My understanding of the rules of faith get all jumbled in my brain, as my heart sings of His Glory! If Jesus could die any day for us, **why that day**? Was there someone who specifically needed Him to be shamed and beaten on that day? Was there someone who needed that particular day, to be the day Jesus hung on the cross? I say YES! There were 2 thieves up there with Him. At first, they both yelled at Jesus and mocked Him. Then one of these losers, who spent his entire life doing wrong and hurting others, had a change of heart. He declared his own guilt and the innocence of Jesus. Next, a step further... *"Jesus, remember me when you come into your Kingdom"*. (*Luke 23:40-43*) Jesus responds with this. *"Truly I tell you, today you will be with me in paradise."*

Could that have happened on any other day in human history? I say NO. Jesus picked that day to suffer and die, because it was also the only time He could get next to a habitual thief and personally give him one last chance!
(*that's my Jesus right there*)

So does my Jesus require a resume'? ... a letter of reference? ... a life of restitution? He didn't then. <u>He didn't even make the guy say the 'sinner's prayer' the right way</u>!!! So what will Jesus accept, for salvation? I believe He is so merciful and kind that He would take the mumbled prayer of a six year old who only came to Sunday School, because he stayed at Grandma's house over night. Even if the rest of that boy's life is wasted and ruined by sin, I believe when he dies, he will appear before the throne of grace and Jesus will be holding a HAHA Contract with a big smile... and open arms.

Do <u>I know</u> that will happen?
No, I do not. Does Jesus love like that? From what I've seen, yes.

      A single moment changed everything for us, the moment Jesus died. Would Jesus accept a single moment in someone's life as salvation, knowing the rest of that person's life would be spent in sin? I only know that **I don't get to make that call** - I will wisely look for fruit, in the lives of those who say they know my King. Fruit means growth and a healthy connection to God. But, I will not judge salvation.

Pictures of Heaven

the evolution of my vision of home

So this is a particularly personal journey of mine. (*it is sort of the way that the Lord has 'evolved' my understanding of my relationship with God and religion in general*)

I think of 'vision' as that thing you keep tucked in your shirt, like soldiers keeps a photo of family close to the heart. It encourages them and makes them keep going so they can finally ...go home.

Okay, so I got saved in 1978 when my Mom brought home a Bible for me from my Grandma's funeral. I loved my Grandma (*Grandma Kate*) and so the Bible held great value to me. It was a small green Gideon's pocket New Testament. In the back was the 'Romans Road' to Salvation. I read it, I believed it and... I got saved. (*thank you Lord*)

I guess **my first picture of Heaven** was like this.. the moment I die, I open my eyes and I'm standing in front of the Pearly Gates, dressed in a white robe. I get on my tippy-toes and try to look over the shoulders of the person in line in front of me. I want to see what it's like inside! (*cute, right?*) I have no fear of not being allowed in (*which was an amazing feeling*). But this picture of Heaven, my first one, was of me still on the outside, the journey only begun, not complete! Me knowing my name was on THE LIST. Showing up, invitation in hand, waiting for some greeter to usher me in. But I was happy with that and now I see that it was the only picture I could handle at the time.

My second picture of Heaven evolved when I went to Bible College. It was 1984 and I had just come to the end of myself. I realized I had become the very kind of guy that I hated most, an epically, self-centered jerk. I fell before God and begged Him to help me learn how to be a better me. (*my soul previously saved, my life was now going to be converted... if that makes sense*) Searching, I found what I needed. A church that told me the two things I needed to hear most, I am unbelievably loved by God <u>and</u> I am a horrible sinner deserving nothing at all, ever! I needed both, not just one. The very conflict of the 2 statements can ease a guilty conscience. (*just ask John Newton*)

I am in Bible College and I'm learning all kinds of Bible-y stuff. My understanding of Heaven is growing, changing and shifting a bit to one side (*the place I attended was a bit on the "we're right, everyone else is wrong" side, I just didn't know that then*). But, God is gentle and good and I see why He let me go there. I met some of my best, life-long friends there and got to start my journey in children's ministry under and along side some truly inspiring people.

That being said, this next picture of Heaven was of me in a long white robe, standing piously in the choir stands... about halfway back. Worshipping my God with all the other chosen saints! (*it was like a religious postcard or something*) Yes, it was a bit of a privileged viewpoint. Not actually based on Jesus' example at all. But it too, made me happy and now I see that it was the only picture I could handle at the time.

My third picture of Heaven came several years later. I can't be sure when, so for that I am sorry. I was married and had two wonderful children by then. I had been working a few different jobs and grown to be a more well-rounded individual. Less Bible-y, I guess you'd say a bit more worldly. Definitely more social, so my picture of Heaven was now also more social too.

I die, open my eyes and BAM, I am standing on the streets of Heaven. Surrounded by all kinds of people I never met. There is an air of anticipation and we're all smiling from ear to ear, waiting for Jesus to address us! I guess in some ways, it is a large jump from the previous pictures I had. No longer focused on rigid piety. No places we're assigned to stand, no choir bleachers and no robes (*just white shirts and pants*) and no gathering of the 'us, not them'. I guess I had more understanding that Jesus will save how and who He saves (*and He's not going to check His list with me*).

A small adjustment but a needed one and this picture of Heaven made me happy and now I see that it was the only picture I could handle at the time.

My next picture of Heaven came (*sadly*) during my divorce. I lost my wife and kids, my place at church, my house, nearly all my friends and even my identity as a man. (*I won't explain any more than that, I have no desire to defend myself or accuse others*) I sank emotionally lower than I ever thought I could. I was lonely, the eating Christmas dinner by myself at Denny's kind of lonely. But Jesus was with me, sitting beside me, telling me He was sorry I was feeling that way. This was the season of my life when I started calling Him, MY Jesus. He went from being a God who loves all of humanity, to My God, companion, kind, patient and completely focused on me. He never said 'I told you so' or looked down on me with folded arms. He became MY Jesus! Though my heart was broken and my joy was gone, He was WITH me. Really, really with ME!!!

My picture of Heaven was now filled with passion and intimacy (*which I had no idea was missing before*). I die and open my eyes standing on the streets of Heaven, unaware of what anyone is wearing. I look around quick and see where Jesus is, in the distance surrounded by others and they are all laughing. (*laughing! that's new*) I start running, pushing people out of the way and head straight for the one I have to see, MY Jesus! As I get close, He turns to face me and I see His eyes, those wells of kindness. I grab him and hug Him like I've waited my whole life to meet Him. (*to be honest, I have told some friends that if they're in my way, standing between me and MY Jesus when I get there, expect an elbow to the side of the head or a kick to the back of the knee to get them out of my way. I told them it's not personal, I just need to get to MY Jesus*) The picture ends and I still haven't let go. I got it now, my picture is personal. I'm not one of the chosen masses, I am Russ and Jesus died for me.

In spite of all the sorrow of that season, the picture of Heaven made me happy, really happy and now I see that it was the only picture I could handle at the time.

My current picture of Heaven is because I asked a silly question. Several years after my divorce.... happily remarried and living in Florida, my second chance at love and church was paying off in the most amazing way. I was really happy! Serving a lot in church, loving my new situation, feeing supremely loved by MY Jesus. Then one day it hit me, I love him more than I ever did before, more than I love anyone or anything else... but nothing like THE WAY HE LOVES ME. Could MY Jesus actually be as excited to see me in Heaven, as I will be to see Him? Obviously, we know that He is, I had just never pictured it before. That was now going to change. A new vision flashed.

I die and open my eyes on the streets of Heaven. My heart is racing, I have to find my Jesus. I turn around and see those kind eyes right in front of me and before I can say, "Thank you", He scoops me up in the warmest, strongest hug... EVER! I cry and melt, because He ran to me. My Jesus ran to see me!!!!!!!!!!!!! As if **HIS picture of Heaven** just had to have ME in it. This picture of Heaven makes me more than happy and I can't imagine any better picture, though I know my romantic God just loves to show off and surprise me.

(obviously, this is fiction, I have no idea of what it will be like, these are just my crazy changing pictures of Heaven, from my journey with Jesus) Though Heaven, for me, is anywhere that's 'me and MY Jesus'. (and you're all invited too)

I hope you have your own evolving vision of Heaven. Growth and change are both signs of a healthy walk with God - If you don't have a vision of heaven, stop right now and ask Jesus to show you what you mean to Him, ask Him for a vision to tuck inside your shirt, ask Him for a vision that will sustain you and whisper hope on your heart when it's growing cold. Ask Him if His vision of Heaven is having you there with Him and He will convince you that He would run to you too!

The accumulation of un-magical days

This is personal, but can be applied in many areas of our lives... so, let's get right to it.

When my kids were little, I was very busy with family, work, ministry and finding myself. Looking back, I was too busy with all that 'good stuff'. My two wonderful kids were little and I often looked for special opportunities to make moments together a huge deal. One such example was around my son's 7th birthday. He had just gotten some money in the mail and finally had enough to buy the toy he had been longing for, the Optimal Optimus Transformer! It was impressive, hard to find and he really wanted. It was a long day at school and we could only go to the store after dinner, as long as his Mom was ok with it.

So we head to the closest store that would carry it and they don't have it. The salesman there suggests we drive to their sister store almost a half hour away. This other store was scheduled to close about the time we would get there. We hopped in the car and drove there. We ran up to the door just as the manager was locking it. I banged on the door and asked him, "Please, we will only take 3 minutes. We want just one special toy." My son lost hope and started to sob. (*it was one of those 'I-just-lost-my-puppy' cries*) The manager opened the door and said, "ok but it has to be quick". We bolted toward the toy section, ran down the transformer aisle and it wasn't there. My son started to ask me if I saw it and I said no. Then it occurred to me, check the end caps, maybe the new-expensive-super-cool toys are there. It was about the third end cap I checked, I picked it up from the bottom shelf and called my son. He came running and his eyes lit up! (*I still love that moment*) I handed him the box and we ran toward the register. As he paid for the toy of his dreams, we both thanked every store employee we saw. We got outside, the manager waved as he locked the door, and we yelled for joy as he gripped the box with all of his might. We had triumphed as a team that night, father and son against evil and boredom and hopelessness. The prize was a toy yes, but I also thought that somehow the prize would be a memory so big and strong of my Dad-ly victory, that my son and I would always be close, he would always fall back on that memory as proof of my love for him. At this moment, my son hasn't spoken to me with even a drop of affection in years. Obviously, that event was only momentous... to me.   (*on to my other child*)

My daughter was in Jr. High and she loved playing volleyball. She loved the other kids from church but quite often was left out of their gatherings and trips because she wasn't on the same coolness level. She just wasn't ever invited to the Youth Pastor's head table at camp or on the fun missions trips. Often, she was only sought out by those kids when it suited them. (*as someone to cover for them while they were doing other things*) At least, that's how it looked to me.

It was the week of church convention, when all the affiliated churches came to town and there was a week of intense fellowship and Bible teaching. The big guns all gathered and the really cool kids all went on trips together that week. Amusement parks, dinners, pool parties... all in part, paid for by running a 'youth concession stand', which, on the days of the big trips, had to be manned by the less popular kids. But as I said, that's how it appeared to me. Now, my daughter was pretty good at pushing folks away at times, she isn't all cupcakes and unicorns, she has a lot of Viking and vinegar in her. So, this particular year when they asked her to cover for them at the concession stand, I bought a brand new volleyball and asked everyone who was going on the trip to sign it and give it to my daughter as a gift for helping. When she got it, WOW she loved it. She felt really appreciated and like she was saving the team by working for them. She felt loved and not forgotten.

Win for the Dad team right? I didn't tell her that it was all my idea and my money, because it meant more coming from them. I don't know if she still thinks it was their idea or not. The point is I aimed for moments, events and the winning 3-pointer. I figured they counted the most, but in hindsight, it was always the accumulation of un-magical days that plants the most seeds, waters the most thoughts and grows the deepest roots. Regular days, not birthdays, holidays or brief shining moments, are what love and faith and hope are built of. What I did was kind and thoughtful, but not monumental. My daughter and I have a very broken relationship at this point in time. I hope it will heal into something new and wonderful soon, but for now, real communicating is hard for us both.

The thing with monuments is...

they don't get built over night! Sure the unveiling happens in one big fantastic moment, but the planning and building takes a lot of uncelebrated days,

...an accumulation of un-magical days.

Those were a few of the events I was so proud to orchestrate in the lives of my kids and I still hold onto them at times in my heart and say, *"but I did this huge thing that time. Why don't you love me?"* Honestly, I was a much better Dad than I am currently admitting to and I tried to be their cheerleader in all things. I only write this because I somehow thought the 'special events' would count for much more than they really did and perhaps, you might have counted on them too. There are too many things in life that we expect to win in moments of splendor.

So what about God and us? Here's two questions;
1) Are we <u>asking for</u> the big magical, miraculous moments and waiting on just them to win our hearts deeper to God? If so, then we will fall and cry, *"you weren't there for me God! I asked for this special thing and you dropped the ball!!"* If we stop asking for the big things we want and ask Him to reveal to us the little things He already does, our hearts will be primed to lean on Him and His faithfulness, even when we don't get what we want. Even if we lose a battle. We will have already seen Him establish Himself as our closest companion during the accumulation of un-magical days. ON

REGULAR DAYS, ...He sits beside us when we're feeling lost (*He's not barking out directions*), He cries with us when we are broken (*He never says I told you so*) and He knows we are better than we think we are (*He made us in His own amazing image*). That is what He does, all day, on every regular, un-magical day. The accumulation of these days and this knowledge, when we are willing to see it, is what wins us to the core! Those other events are just Him... showing off and embarrassing us with His romance.

The harder question is...

2) Are we <u>only offering</u> God the special events that we can fit into our schedules and not the multitude of our regular days?

"Lord, didn't I do this or give that? I led that Bible study and gave to the hungry kids that time!" Are we a people who give to God like He's a homeless God that we feed Thursday nights, or are we seeking His companionship with every new morning, <u>even when we feel like there's nothing to offer Him but the broken version of us</u>? Here's the real surprise in this, He reveals something wondrous to us when we give Him our accumulated un-magical days. He reveals a love for us that makes no sense, needs no ribbons or presents, doesn't depend on our efforts at all and somehow makes the regular into something more than magical!

The accumulation of un-magical days is where the greatest victories are found, the strongest faith is revealed and the truest of loves are proven!

10 spoons

Did you ever get food delivered?

You know, like for a bunch of people... maybe a couple of platters of sandwiches or pans of pasta? Hopefully the people you ordered from gave you a lot of silverware in the bags too. You might not have told the person who took your order that you were feeding ten or twenty, but they probably figured it out by the amount of food you ordered. <u>The volume of food should suggest the number of mouths</u>. Now, when you go to Grandma's house for the holidays and you are helping to set the table, the same principle works in reverse. You say, "Hey Grandma, how many place settings do we need?" She might say seven or she might say seventeen. This information then makes you picture how many chairs will be needed and even how much food she is probably cooking. Makes sense right? The volume of food suggests the number of mouths and the number of settings suggests the volume of food.

I am here to tell you that you were given ten spoons by God! God never intended us to just take care of ourselves (*Gen 4:9 - am I my brother's keeper?*). He also never intended to give us 'just enough' (*John 10:10 - abundant life*). What God intended was life <u>overflowing</u> with love and peace and hope. (*not money, just the important things*) He intended us to have dominion over creation, on His behalf. Just and kind co-rulers, sharing the responsibility and the joy together!!!! Yup, that was the plan for all of us in the garden of Eden. Oh and IT IS STILL THE PLAN.

Say what???? Yes, it's still God's plan for us. I call this '10 spoons' because it makes me think of a huge pot of chili, <u>a pot made for sharing</u>.
When I make chili, I always double the meat and beans and the chopped up green peppers and onions. To me, chili is more than comfort food. It's an event. HAHA Yes, making

chili is a special event to me and I love to share it. *"Here, try some. Do you want shredded cheese or sour cream with it? BOTH?? ME TOO! Fritos, here, you gotta have Fritos with the chili as well."* When I make chili, I also make sure that there are enough bowls and spoons to go around. I want to make sure that anybody who wants some, gets some.

Like I said, <u>I make chili to share</u>.

I believe God made fruit trees that way too. Honestly, how many mangos does the tree really need to make, to replace itself? But have you seen a huge mango tree??? Tons and tons of mangos!!! Enough mangos to plant seeds, to eat and to share with all the neighbors. That is God's intended picture of us. God gave us 10 spoons. It's the 'heads-up' that the volume we are supposed to be getting from God is too much to hoard, too much to keep to ourselves. God is a fountain, a spring of (*life-giving*) fresh water, flowing and flowing and flowing! Not just a drizzle. We are vessels, containers for His outpouring. Being made in His image, we are supposed to be outpouring too.

He fills us so we can also pour out.
(let me put to rest the 2 objections that come up most)

1. There is no chance of Him running out
2. If we hoard what He gives us, it will become stagnant, stale and rotten. Lifeless.

The devil and our sin-poisoned flesh tell us these things can't possibly be true, but Jesus turned off His God-stuff as He walked the earth and relied solely on His Heavenly Father, knowing that we would need that example. He, who was the fountain, became a vessel like us. As a vessel, He fed 5000 and said we would do greater things. I think we all do that thing where we think about 'how much we need', when we are confronted with the choice to be generous. A homeless person asks us for cash and we sort of reach in our pockets trying not to take everything out, only what we don't need. Right? Well, that is not God's plan. He intended us to have dominion over creation, on His behalf. <u>Just and kind co-rulers, sharing the responsibility and the joy together</u>!

God gave us each 10 spoons to remind us of how He provides. If we give away what He gave us, He will give us more. (*Talents, money, compassion, clothes, hope, tears, joy and time*) They're all meant to be shared, like a harvest. That's why love, joy, peace, patience, kindness, goodness, faithfulness, gentleness and self-control are the **fruit** of the Holy Spirit!

- He fills us so we can pour out -

Backpack full of rocks

I have a concept that I have used repeatedly in my life, to help me avoid bitterness and cultivate thankfulness. It is called 'a backpack full of rocks'. (*it closely follows the 'don't throw the baby out with the bath water' idea, but with a bit more explanation*)

When faced with something unpleasant or difficult, I try to think of it like this. Each season, each adventure, places a bunch of rocks in my backpack. Some are good and some are bad. They become the weight or burden, of my season. I carry them with me as I travel each day. When I have a season of intense disappointment or even a season of great regret, the weight of that season seems to get overwhelming and bog me down. The key is this, I have to **stop**, take off the backpack and **go through all the rocks**. The bad rocks get thrown out and the good rocks get put back in my backpack for me to continue carrying on my journey.

I have to say that I believe that carrying some burdens can be very healthy for us in our walk with God. Isn't knowing, the death that Jesus bore in His body for us, a kind of burden? Sure there is great joy because of it, but the agony He went through and how often we fail, in spite of that amazing grace can be the burden of being undeserving and keep us tethered to our Savior, if kept in proper balance. So I gladly carry the good rocks, the good burdens with me on my journey. In my mind, they are like building a stone altar in the Old Testament, to remind me of the wondrous things God has done. I carry that stone altar with me.

Years ago, I belonged to a church that did some really bad things to a lot of people. This is true and it put a lot of bad rocks in my backpack. While I was with this church, I learned a lot of Bible truth, served with some of the best people I've ever met and had experiences that changed me for the better. This is true and it put a lot of good rocks in my backpack. Since then I have talked with many people who, at some point, just took the backpack off and laid it on the side of the road. They put it down and walked away, they walked away from ALL the rocks and they walked away from God! I understand the hurt and disappointment, the disgust and weariness from that part of their journey. There was a lot of bad, a lot of lies and a lot that can weigh down our hearts. But if I drop the entire bag and all of the rocks, I deny the good things as well and make a huge place for bitterness, denying and <u>rejecting</u> the things I can be thankful for. <u>Those good things are like a dandelion growing up through a sidewalk. They're a spark of wild life that God somehow threaded through the unyielding rock of manmade dishonor</u>.

Here's my advice to everyone carrying a backpack full of burdens that make their knees weaker with every step. Step over to the side of your path, have a seat and pull the backpack off your shoulders. Place it right in front of you and unzip it. Pull out one rock, look it over and decide if it is a good rock or a bad rock. Do this **one rock at a time** and understand that each rock is either bad or good, never both. If you grab a rock and it looks like both, turn it around and look it over until you find the crack line in it and break it apart so it's split into both a good rock and a bad rock. I will give you one of my examples. The Bible doctrine I was taught in college seemed like a rock that was both good (*learning God's truth*) and bad (*using God's truth to oppress people*). I had to take that one out and look for the crack so I could separate those two things. In this case, <u>the crack in it was Jesus</u>! I had to look at the way He used truth to love people and draw them, not condemn them and break them. Once I found that spot. I pushed my thumbs in there and POP, two rocks, one good, one bad. I looked at the good rock and thought about how much of God's Word was given to me there, I was rich in knowledge. The bad rock was seeing how people can use this wonderful knowledge to do the work of the devil. Keep the good rock throw the bad one away!

Bad rock? How they put people into cliques and promoted those who agreed with them and made them look good.

Good rock? How some folks I met made time for everyone, even the really annoying people! HAHA... like me

Bad rock? Seeing people evangelize with fear tactics and intimidation so they could have a higher numbers of converts.

Good rock? Seeing workers in the children's ministry laughing and being kind to the kids they were entrusted with.

Keep the good rock throw the bad one away!

Go through the entire bag until it's empty, put the good rocks back in and <u>walk away from the rest</u>. This works in relationships, jobs, ministries, anything. It's never, all bad. God doesn't leave us with all bad.

When I was going through my separation and divorce, there were an awful lot of bad rocks, (*and they were heavy*) but there were good ones too. There were a few people that treated me with love and kindness, not as many as said they would, only a few. That is a very good rock. I also learned how to be empathetic and compassionate to others going through divorces, also a very good rock. My closeness with my Jesus grew incredibly intimate, GREAT ROCK!!! I kept them and now when I remember that horrible season, I have a few really good rocks that make me smile! That season has purpose and value much more than agony and sorrow I went through at the time. It's sacred now!

Whatever it is in your backpack that is weighing you down, please don't just throw it all away, sit down and go through it, cry it out and separate the good from the bad. In that way, we bring honor and value to that season and it becomes a sacred landmark of the wondrous things that God has done!

I yell at God

I admit it, I sometimes yell at God. It's not out of anger at God or out of disrespect. Honestly, when I yell at God, I am doing it to help myself.

Let me back up. I know God is Holy and to be feared (*approached with reverence/respect*). He is also my personal Father and He adores me. He knows all my good traits and my bad ones and I firmly believe that God enjoys me. Just as Jesus enjoyed the knuckleheads that walked with Him! That's why I'm pretty sure that God smiles when I yell at Him.

I am currently not very close with my kids. Not by choice, but because of circumstances. Some are of my own making and some I still don't understand. I love both of my kids beyond measure, but don't know how to fix the gap between us. One of my kids talks to me occasionally, the other, not at all. The conversations are never really the ones I want to have. No chatting about God's faithfulness or what He's been speaking into our lives or how we can serve together in the future. Just non-eternal stuff. I am thankful for that though, at least it's something.

There are days when it gets to me real bad. Days when I cry and cry and cry. I miss my kids and I miss what I think we could be having together. Obviously, I would never interfere with free-will, so I wait for ...I'm not sure what, perhaps a miracle, perhaps more directions, perhaps the balm of time and the forgiveness it may bring. So when it really hurts too much, I yell at God. I yell because of the pain in my heart and the noise in my head. I yell so I can hear something good over the loneliness and hopelessness inside.

I know some of you are probably thinking I should just put on some Jesus music and think on good things or maybe pray and meditate on God's Word. All good and wise council! Seriously, those are wise things I do! However, there are times when grief has to be dealt with, carried, felt and not just covered over. Even King David expressed his overwhelming sorrow in the Psalms, along with his declarations of who and what he needed God to be for him in those seasons. In his own way, David yelled at God.

I yell, because God is the one who's help I need. God is the one who's proven Himself faithful, capable, willing. God is who my hope rests in! I yell at God. I know He hears. I know He cares. I know He feels my pain. I know that only He can do something to fix this. I also know that if His plan doesn't include fixing it while I'm alive, He'll carry me when I can no longer stand because of the heartache!

What do I yell? I yell what I know and what I believe about God. I declare His mercy and His kindness on my behalf. What I yell is personal and it's what I need to know at that moment.

"God, you are great and powerful! God you are good and kind! You adore me and I expect you to prove it again!! If you won't fix this and let me have my Kids in my life, then I expect you to give them back to me in heaven!! I expect you to be who you are and chase them Lord, chase my kids hard and catch them!!! That's what you do God!!! Get them to you! I will keep following you, I will do what you have for me to do, because you're going to do what you do best fix this!!!!!"

When I yell at God, I am saying things with force, things that I know about God. I am declaring His strength and integrity. I am declaring His faithfulness and goodness. I am reminding myself who it is that's writing my story. My God is an author who loves surprise happy endings! When I yell at God, I am telling Him that I expect Him to be God.

That is when my soul finds peace and I can go on. Yell if you have to, His love can take it!

The string, the kite and the wind

I sometimes think of my wife and I as the string and the kite. She is pragmatic, factual and practical. I am optimistic, a dreamer and a chance taker. In our relationship, she is the string and I am the kite. Now, to some, this may seem like an excuse or an insulting statement, but it isn't. I am not saying that either of us is right or wrong, in fact, we work very well together. I tend to encourage her to reach for the stars and look beyond apparent limitations. She tends to keep me grounded in facts and on schedule, when I'd probably get us into debt over a whim. Most times, she is the string and I am the kite.

If this were a children's book I would point out two important things. Without the kite, the string would never see the sky and without the string, the kite would be lost and ruined. Can you picture the two becoming friends in the book? A kite with a goofy smile, trying to jump off of logs and cliffs to fly. He's always dirty and banged up. The string is this crumply squiggle with glasses on, always looking down, watching where she's going, so she doesn't trip. Then they meet and listen to each other's dreams. "I want to be free", the kite says. "I want to be safe", the string says. Not knowing that they need each other to reach their dreams.

The string tries to convince the kite that he should change his dream to a more sensible one. The kite tries to convince the string that she should change her dream to something more fun. **Neither is meant to convince the other to change**.

Along comes the wind and whispers, "help each other". The string tells the kite her idea. "I will hold onto you with all my might and you jump into the sky as high as you can!"

The wind smiles at the plan and begins to blow. The string holds onto the kite with one end and the kite jumps as hard as he can. '*Whooosh*', the wind comes rushing in and catches the kite as it had so many other times. The kite thinks, "Oh no, here I go, the wind will throw me around and

I will crash to the ground again". The string feels a tug, no a pull. A definite pull! Geessh!!!!! A really strong pull. She reaches for a tree with her other end and wraps around it. She stretches and stretches as far as she can.

......*you can picture it, right?*

By allowing the string to hold him down, the kite finally soared.

By holding the kite down, the string was finally lifted up!

The point is this, I did not know that I needed my Sweety to hold me down so I could soar and she didn't know that in holding onto me, she would reach new heights.

God knew though!

I believe that we take turns in this life. Some days we are the kite, some days we are the string. Every day, we need each other to complete our purposes. Lead or support? <u>God forbid we think we are only supposed to do one or the other</u>.

As for the wind, obviously it's the Holy Spirit!

When you find yourself struggling with your 'purpose in life' and you aren't getting your answers from God, stop, take a breath and consider this. Perhaps today is your string day? Maybe God is waiting for you to assist someone else with their dreams before He moves on to fulfilling yours!

Zech 4:10 *"...who hath despised the day of small things?"*
...for His economy is very different from ours!!!

You picked those guys?

Normally, when picking teams, you go for the folks who have the skills and talents that will lead to victory. Ok, so you might pick a friend because you're close to them or pick someone because they are cute, but mostly you will pick those best suited to giving you the win. Anyone who is trying to accomplish something would probably agree with that strategy. You should pick for your team carefully and make it those best suited to giving you the win.

The problem is, Jesus threw **that strategy** away and went after a bunch of knuckleheads. He chose a tax collector, a rebellious bunch of fishermen and Judas, who wanted Jesus to be something other than what He was. We are going to drop Judas from the discussion, since he chose to leave the group. The other 11 were not criminals really, maybe minor stuff, brawling, drinking and the tax collector who was considered a traitor by the other Jews. **Lord, that's like the worst choices ever for a winning team!!!** The thing is, Jesus didn't want a team that would excel right off the bat. He didn't want those who make it look easy. He wanted those who would struggle and fail, just like us. He wanted us to have roll models that didn't set the bar too high for us, regular human beings with doubts and fears of their own, that they needed to overcome.
Examples we could follow!

Here's my way of picturing it...
Imagine you have to crawl under barbed wire through a huge patch of mud. Life can seem like that with all the troubles we face. So who is going to be more helpful to most folks with getting through this obstacle? Someone dressed in a leader's uniform standing on the outside barking orders? (*honestly, that wouldn't help me very much, I might just go through it so I can punch them in the head*) How about someone about 3 to 6 feet in front of you, going through the

same thing, looking back at you with a smile saying, "*C'mon, you got this, just stay with me and we'll make it through together.*" Yea, that's the kind of leader I like to follow. If I can see someone go through the same thing I'm going through, then I can have hope that it's possible for me too. YES, I know that God already said I can do all things through Him and He makes me more than a conqueror and all that, but let's be honest, there are times when the promises feel unattainable. Our hearts get tired, our joy fades and it all seems impossible. We are human, we are broken, and we are self-defeating puddles of sin and confusion. We are also deeply loved and romantically pursued by the Creator of the Universe. So, He gave us examples of those He calls faithful and heroes. Examples that are knuckleheads, just like us.

Do I need to remind you who took this path before us?

Peter: impulsive, moody, denying and scared to do what Jesus asked Him to do

Thomas: doubting, doubter, doubt-aholic, show me... no prove it to me... fine, I guess it's probably true

Paul: follow the stinking rules or you die, seriously... stone that guy for breaking the rules

James: a temper, smash them Lord for not listening to us.. crush them.. bring down fire

You see, Jesus knows that He personally set the bar way too high for us. He was showing us how far from being righteous and holy we are, so then He calls knuckleheads to be our examples of how to work it out in real time. The more I see my flesh nature warring with the Spirit of God within me, the more thankful I am that the first ones to follow Jesus were arrogant, cowardly, insecure, prideful, wishy-washy, legalistic, stubborn, impulsive, double-minded, confused and prone to wander. (*Just like me*)

What about the things God has asked you to lead or be a part of? Are you trying to be that squeaky-clean, perfect example or are you willing to let those beside you see you crawling through the mud too? As my wife says, "*Salvation is free, discipleship costs you everything!*"

The world already has a perfect example in Jesus, what they need to see is people like you and me, covered in mud, soaked in tears and still trying, still reaching for that high standard and asking, "Lord please give me a boost!"

...Because He picked you and me to be those knuckleheads
for somebody else -

Keep unity, make peace

Semantics is really just a fancy word for the way that words can be used to mean different things or how people can use words to push you into thinking a certain way about something.

Often **unity** is something we try to *make* or encourage.

Likewise, **peace** is something we try to *keep* or maintain.

In both cases, we are not in agreement with the Word of God! So it's worth looking at the subtle differences in the wording between what we usually say or think, and what God has to say about peace and unity. (*I will use only one verse for each to save time*)

In Matthew 5:9 Jesus says, "*blessed are the peacemakers , for they shall be called the children of God.*" Peace MAKERS, not keepers! Here's how I see it, peace keepers usually stop people from hurting each other by getting between them and putting out both arms to separate the angry parties. I know you can picture it, someone on the schoolyard or in the break room with their arms out wide between two people yelling at each other, a palm on each person's chest, holding them back, *'keeping the peace'*. God bless that person for getting involved and wanting the fighting to stop. It's normal to think that the solution would be as simple as putting distance between the arguing parties. But when we look at mankind's situation we can see that peace is something that has to be made.

Mankind in a broken relationship with God, kicked out of the Garden of Eden by the law. What does KEEPING THE PEACE look like? An angel with a flaming sword securing the distance enemies, making sure the <u>fighting was interrupted</u>. (*Genesis 3:24*) **That's a picture of what 'keeping the peace' really is**, just an interruption of the relationship and the fighting. What's really needed isn't an interruption, but <u>restoration</u>!

Jesus loved us so much, He saw the interruption and said, "No, I want to fix it and restore the relationship between God and mankind. Father, let me go down there and make peace!" Peace came with a terrible price. <u>Jesus went to the cross to make peace between God and us</u>! Peace, real peace, not just a pause in fighting. He ended the argument and took away the hostile feelings and even <u>took away the right to be angry</u>. Jesus ended God's right to be angry by paying in full for the sin of all mankind. There was no more debt - That is our example of making peace!

How often do we just interrupt fighting instead of making peace? I get it. It's not my fight. Not my problem. Why should I pay for something that isn't my fault? I guess that's why Jesus says if we go the extra mile and make peace, we will be called <u>the children of God</u>.

I will give you one more example from my life. I adore my wife. She is also too hard on herself at times. Today she needed a Notary Public, which we found nearby. She went in for a one page stamp and signature. She came out with a scowl. When she got in the car she muttered a few things and called herself stupid, because that signature cost ten dollars, when she thought it should have cost two. We are down to the last of our savings and living on prayer and the generosity of friends, so she is very mindful of the money we spend.

I started to encourage her and tell her it was fine and God's got this, but she just said, "I don't want to talk about it". That was the end of the conversation. She didn't want my opinion or God's word, just an interruption... not peace. Several hours later I told her that she needed to make peace and not just tell her 'self-argument' to shut up. We all do that to ourselves! We don't even make peace with (*or for*) ourselves. ***"Self? Yes I'm talking to you! You may not be happy with the outcome to some of your (our) decisions, but I need you to know that God has got this, you didn't do anything wrong. You are not stupid, you are a talented,*** *deeply loved child of God and He doesn't have stupid kids!! So your attitude is incorrect and if you did do anything wrong, it could never be so wrong that the blood of Jesus couldn't take it away. YOU HEAR ME? It's gone, removed from existence. There is nothing to blame you for, so right now, it's like you are gossiping about you. That's just weird so live in the PEACE Jesus made for you to have, with YOU! Hugs and I love you, I mean me...us."* Blessed are the peacemakers... restore everyone, even yourself, because Jesus' blood and love, are that powerful.

'The unity issue' - What we usually do is try to create unity where there is division. The problem here is that when we try to make unity, it means we are agreeing with the definition of division. We see a world around us that acts so divided, so separate. Split into a thousand different groups all calling out for equality. Of course we think the solution is 'making' unity. Forcing everyone to be on the same team by passing laws, lifting signs and creating procedures to promote unity.

In Ephesians 4:3 we are encouraged to, "make every effort to keep the unity of the Spirit through the bond of peace." It's as if God is saying that He already established unity between us. "Keep the unity", KEEP IT, don't let it slip away. Don't trade it. Put in the effort to hold on to it, keep it.

God says that unity is already ours, in the Spirit. (*I see it like this*) God's Spirit tells us we are all related, part of the same family, children of the same God, all created in His image and equals. This is what God says about us so it is true above and over anything the world says. In other words, we are united, we have unity, we are equal, and we are one people under God.

WE ARE!

We have unity already, it's ours and it's in us and we are one people of one purpose. The devil likes to lie to us and say that we are not united, that there is no unity. He can't undo what Jesus did to fix things between God and us so he aims at our relationships with other people. He says we are separate and disconnected and alone.

Us against them!

We get so occupied with the tricks of Satan that we forget the truth of God. When we walk in the Spirit, we reconnect with the truth and realize we have unity and <u>we don't have to fight **to get it**, just endeavor to keep it</u>.

Jesus made peace, the Spirit confirms unity and the flesh believes the lies that God's house is divided. Let's remember our 'Heavenly' family roots and be peacemakers that keep the unity. That is our family tradition, our honor and our privilege.

A squirrel's offering

Quite a few years back, I wanted to get a squirrel costume and ask the head Pastor if I could take the offering.

I would come out on stage all dressed in brown with buck teeth and a bushy tail and address the congregation, something like this. "Hello, my name is Sebastian and... I am a squirrel. If the ushers would get ready for the offering please? Today I will read to you from the book of... (*flipping through my Bible*)... the book of Squirrel, ...chapter 21, please join me there. In this portion, we read the story of the Prodigal Squirrel. Once there was a kind old squirrel with 2 sons. One day as they were gathering nuts to be buried near their tree, the youngest son took a break and went to speak with his father. Father, he said, I am tired of this labor! My friends have all left their trees on this side of the road and gone out to the lands far beyond the other side. This broke the father squirrel's heart for he knew what his son was going to ask. Father, I want to do, what I want to do. Allow me to leave, that I may follow my own dreams and go where my friends are.

Tearfully, the father squirrel crawled over to his youngest son and put his tiny gray paw on his son's shoulder and said, I will miss you and I don't think your decision is very wise, but I love and won't keep you here if you want to go. Are you sure that your friends are safe where they have gone? The young squirrel replied, of course father, if it wasn't as wonderful over there as we hoped, I am sure they would have returned and told me so. May I have your blessing to leave? Sadly the father said go my son, you have my blessing.

It only took a few minutes for the young squirrel to get ready and leave. The father watched as he hopped away... away from their tree, away from home and away from him. The father squirrel's tears fell. Soon the older brother entered the tree to see what had happened. He found his father crying and said, father do not weep for my brother's foolishness, you still have me and I remain faithful. The father looked at his eldest son and smiled.

It was a short time later when the wayward squirrel approached the road that he had longed to cross. He felt his hope leap within him as he stepped out onto the breakdown lane. I will find my friends and we will enjoy a new adventure together, he said to himself. As he approached the center lines of the road, he was amazed to see what looked like some of his friends waiting for him on the far side. He leaned and squinted and saw the torn and shredded carcasses of the squirrels that went before him. I have been a fool, he yelled! I left a home of safety and love for a place I knew nothing of. I will return to my father and tell him that I don't deserve to be his son anymore and I will ask him to forgive me. The frightened squirrel turned and SPLAT... got run over by a truck!" (*close the Bible and look around*) "The End"

You see, squirrels don't have a Savior, only (*pointing a furry paw*)... only YOU do! Of all creation, of all the beautiful things God made, only people have a Savior. In spite of your selfishness, your fears, hatred and fighting. You ignore the needy, you destroy the planet He made for you, you lie, steal and cheat each other... and some how, you... you humans, are His favorite things and His love for you is so great that He gave his son to offer you forgiveness, hope, healing and heaven! I hope your offering today, reflects the unmatched honor He places upon you! There are no second chances for prodigal squirrels. Honestly, I think you humans are the only ones in all of creation, who can't see how special you are to God... and how undeserved that is. Thank you. (*walk off the stage*)

That is how I hope I respond to every day and everything He gives me...

As amazingly undeserved!

Misplaced interference

I am sorry if this topic complicates your relationships. That is not the goal. Realignment is.

Kind of a loaded statement to begin with, I know. This idea came from a talk I had with God concerning my wife. She was going through something physical and it was really wearing her down. Physically, emotionally and spiritually, she was beat up and just so tired. I adore my Sweety and because of that, I want her to be ok all the time. I want to fix whatever's wrong. I think almost all of us would say, "*that's what love is and does.*"

I used to think that way, but now I think that's a little off center. I'm pretty sure Jesus would agree with me on this example. ***The woman caught in adultery***. Jesus forgave her sins and told her to go and sin no more. He didn't fix everything. He fixed something and left the rest up to her. It wouldn't be <u>a second chance</u> to do things right, if someone did it all correctly for you.

1Cor 13:7 LOVE... "*bears all things, believes all things, hopes all things, and endures all things.*" WOW, look at that, it didn't mention FIXES ALL THINGS. Love doesn't take away responsibility, it doesn't remove all sources of hurt and it doesn't get in the way of needing God. That's our big point in all this, the 'need for God'. When your spouse or child is in pain, you may accidentally remove their need for God, or at least block it. Our emotions are so attached to their happiness and well being that, if they are suffering, it can reflect on us as if we failed or aren't caring enough. We can interpret their pain as us being a bad parent or spouse. We often find ourselves thinking, "what am I doing wrong? Aren't I doing enough?"

As a wise friend used to say, life is full of 'life'. There is pain, disappointment, hurt, anger, abuse, rejection, prejudice and a million other problems in every life. They may be wrapped in differing circumstances, but when opened, hurt is hurt, no matter who you are. Thankfully, we don't have to face these things alone, because God is near to the broken hearted! I'm not making that up, it's in the Bible. Ps 34:18 *"The Lord is near to the brokenhearted and saves the crushed in spirit."*

I also like the version in the Message Bible, *"If your heart is broken, you'll find God right there; if you're kicked in the gut, he'll help you catch your breath."* THAT is the opportunity that sorrow and suffering brings to each of us, the chance to see God right there, the chance to have Him personally help us catch our breath! Oh, the intimacy that God can and wants to bring into our hurts. He doesn't create the hurts, sin does and we do. He just stays near us waiting for us to lean on Him so He can roll up His sleeves and express His wild love. He may express it in hope or comfort or turning situations around or bottling our tears, but He will express it if we let Him. THAT is exactly what we interfere with 'because of love'. We get in the way of God keeping His most intimate promises to our loved ones. Are we trying to take God's place in their lives? Or worse, <u>are we secretly saying that we can't trust God to love them better than we do</u>?

Please, if you love someone, stop cutting off God's chance to meet their needs, to develop their patience or strengthen their character! It's just limiting their relationship with God.

Do you know what love really does?
Love trusts God to make things right, His way and in His time.
Don't destroy someone's ability to need God!

Let go of your faith

(I asked Millie if she thought the phrase had a negative connotation or a positive one and she said negative... I said good, thank you - I like when I see things in a new light)

Here's the positive version of 'let go of your faith'! I admit that I spent a few decades thinking of my faith as a tool I used in my life. It wasn't a conscious decision, just more of a religious-cultural implication that I guess I grew up with. Honestly, I see how it makes sense that as a person, my faith is my choice and as my choice, I can display it any way that I want to. I can put it on a t-shirt or car sticker, I can wear it as a necklace or tattoo, I can use it to direct my voting or vocabulary. It's mine... it's my choice! If I use it only when it suits me or tuck it away until Sunday that's fine because... it's my faith, my choice. I can use it as a defense for myself or as a judgment on others. I can use my faith to pick my friends or pick my enemies. It's mine and I can use it however and whenever I want!   I OWN IT!!!

Unless I misunderstood what my faith is supposed to be.

I do get to choose my faith. That is true. It's part of the 'free-will' design God gave us and it is a very sacred honor indeed. Here's the problem, what if (*hold on tight*), what if our faith is supposed to be in control of us? What if we aren't supposed to use it, but <u>be used by it</u>?
(Read it again out loud with me please)

What if we aren't supposed to use our faith, but be used by it?

Jesus did tell Peter that when he was older, he would be lead (*by the Spirit of God*) where he would not want to go (Jn 21:18)

It seems to me that we tend to keep our faith on a leash or in a jar. Continually shaping it a bit. Limiting it. Reigning it back in. We love displaying it, <u>properly of course</u>, as defined by the culture of our choice. Like a groomed dog pranced around and offered little yum-yums for best behavior! Is our faith on a leash, never allowed to run wild? Could it be that we really need a faith that frightens us a bit, as it runs happily to explore. A faith that takes off and forces us to chase it, leaving us bent over and out of breathe, far from where we were comfortable and safe?

I can see the terror in that, placing my whole trust in something I can't control at all. **An Unleashed Faith!!!** It seems more natural to set some limits on this wild creature... impose a few restrictions, you might say... <u>domesticate it</u>. Seems fair. I did pick it from the other options out there. You adopt a dog, you can pick it's name and decide if it's a working dog, a lap dog or one of those 'take you everywhere in a stroller' dogs. Is it the same way with faith? Keep what you want and throw out the rest? Isn't that what Lucifer did or tried to do? Honestly, if we get to define our own faith, aren't we just usurping God's authority? *"We know best, we'll make the decisions about right and wrong, good and evil, thanks anyway though."*

Jesus isn't the example of how people should <u>treat me</u> ...He's the example of how I should live and treat others! Let go of your faith, cut the cord, drop the leash, whatever... just let your faith lead for a change. Follow it to the treasures of surrender. A faith that fits into my life will need to be bent and trimmed to be complimentary. <u>A lovely adjective for my story</u>. The faith Jesus spoke of... well, it takes over and we find ourselves <u>adrift in it</u>, no longer the main character in our own story!!!   - That frightens us -   What if I never find my way back to being in control?

or more accurately...

What if God uses me how He wants to, for the rest of my life??

(*That possibility absolutely thrills and frightens me*)

We can be the example for someone who's scared. We can be those footprints in the snow, confirming that this path has been taken before. All hope is not lost! We can be heroes in someone's family tree, prompting a trailblazer, another Abram who hears a heavenly voice calling his or her name!!!

Let go of your faith. Let it lead you. Maybe that's what all our choices really boil down to, faith or fear. Which will lead you? If you have your faith on a leash, look close at the small print on that leash, it might say 'made of 98% Fear and 2% Polyester'.

Let go of your Faith

What if God invites me to do something dangerous? What if it's something hard or painful or if He asks me to give up what I have? We often think it's better, more practical, more responsible to put our faith on a leash! The problem is, in light of the cross that Jesus died on, it also sounds limited and selfish and it sounds like me.

Why would I want a faith that sounds like me?

Isn't that the reason for faith? To be changed into the best version of ourselves?

Let go of your faith, if it's real, <u>it will hold onto you</u>!

Magic words

We probably all grew up being taught that the magic words are PLEASE and THANK YOU.

These are the words that open doors for us, our expressions of humility and gratitude. *Please* is supposed to come before every request. As an act of honoring the one whom you want to receive from. *Thank you* is supposed to follow every answered request, honoring the one who gave you what you asked for. It's simple really, be nice and you can get what you need. I think we can all agree that is how life is supposed to work right?

Well, then there's JESUS. He changes all the rules. He changes the bad rules and even the good rules. Yes, Jesus changed the GOOD RULES! He gave **freely** to everyone. (*To those who were kind and those who were not*) He gave because He loved. Loved like a no one had ever seen before. His type of love had nothing to do with manners or even how things are supposed to work. He said in Luke 6:27-36...

"But I tell you who hear me: Love your enemies, do good to those who hate you, bless those who curse you, pray for those who mistreat you. If someone strikes you on one cheek, turn to him the other also. If someone takes your cloak, do not stop him from taking your tunic. Give to everyone who asks you, and if anyone takes what belongs to you, do not demand it back. Do to others as you would have them do to you. If you love those who love you, what credit is that to you? Even 'sinners' love those who love them. And if you do good to those who are good to you, what credit is that to you? Even 'sinners' do that. And if you lend to those from whom you expect repayment, what credit is that to you? Even 'sinners' lend to 'sinners,' expecting to be repaid in full. But love your enemies, do good to them, and lend to them without expecting to get anything back. Then your reward will be great, and you will be sons of the Most High, because he is kind to the ungrateful and wicked. Be merciful, just as your Father is merciful."

The thing about Jesus is, He meant exactly what He said. To bring the point home, He lived it out Himself, right in front of everyone. Even the good rules were blown out of the water. It was like He was bringing in a new reality! Redefining fair and friend and love and right... everything! So our magic words got high-jacked!!!! No longer please and thank you. No longer if you're nice, then you get stuff. No longer you better be grateful or you get no more. The new magic words are GRACE and MERCY. (*Simple definitions: Grace: getting the good things that you don't deserve, Mercy: not getting the bad things that you do deserve*)

There's not supposed to be any **'if, then'** about me and you EVER AGAIN. Now, it's about me and God or you and God and that's all we are supposed to be dealing with. It's not **if** you are, **then** I will. It's now 'since God did, I will!' Say it with me, "**SINCE GOD DID, I WILL**".

What if those became our new magic words? Well, obviously it would make the world a kinder and better place, but look at Luke 6, verses 35 and 36 again.. "But love your enemies, do good to them, and lend to them without expecting to get anything back. Then your reward will be great, and you will be sons of the Most High, because he is kind to the ungrateful and wicked. Be merciful, just as your Father is merciful."

Think of it like this, it's not a suggestion or promise. It's a fact. Jesus changed all the rules and if we are on His team, we should be playing by those new rules too.

Limited offering

In the Old testament, people gave God offerings. Let's go back to the first one mentioned outside of the Garden of Eden. Gen 4:1-8 *"Adam made love to his wife Eve, and she became pregnant and gave birth to Cain. She said, "With the help of the Lord I have brought forth a man." Later she gave birth to his brother Abel.*

Now Abel kept flocks, and Cain worked the soil. In the course of time Cain brought some of the fruits of the soil as an offering to the Lord. And Abel also brought an offering—fat portions from some of the firstborn of his flock. The Lord looked with favor on Abel and his offering, but on Cain and his offering He did not look with favor. So Cain was very angry, and his face was downcast.

Then the Lord said to Cain, "Why are you angry? Why is your face downcast? If you do what is right, will you not be accepted? But if you do not do what is right, sin is crouching at your door; it desires to have you, but you must rule over it." Now Cain said to his brother Abel, "Let's go out to the field." While they were in the field, Cain attacked his brother Abel and killed him."

The first kids ever born and the oldest murders his brother.

Now I have to back up a few verses to look at a very important point. It says, *The Lord looked with favor on Abel and his offering, <u>but on Cain and his offering He did not look with favor.</u> So Cain was very angry, and his face was downcast.*

You might be tempted to think this whole issue was God's fault, for not being pleased with the offering that Cain brought. Here is what we know about God: He is more interested in our hearts than our stuff. He didn't need either of their offerings. He didn't need food at all. So He wasn't rejecting WHAT CAIN BROUGHT, He was <u>probably</u> rejecting HOW HE BROUGHT IT. Perhaps Cain was too prideful about what he brought or dishonest about it or maybe Cain was thinking, 'if I give God this stuff, then I can do the bad stuff that I want to do and He'll have to forgive me'. I'm not sure what was inappropriate about Cain's offering but God did say to Him, *"If you do what is right, will you not be accepted? But if you do not do what is right, sin is crouching at your door; it desires to have you, but you must rule over it"*. It really is more about how we give, than what we give.

A heart that's right with God, humble, appreciative and ready to be taught. THAT is what He wants most from us. Why does He want that from us? Actually He wants that WITH us. **It's a perfect fit**! He is good and great and always right. He's generous and kind. He's ready and eager to lead us to our best life and the best version of us! So, if we are humble, appreciative and ready to be taught, this pairing between Him and us is a glorious and miraculous thing! It's not so much God's demand. It's more like His offer to us. If we can make ourselves available to God fully, then He can fully share all that he has for us. Perfect fit -

Look at the examples in scripture. Psalm 51:16-17 "For You do not delight in sacrifice, otherwise I would give it; You are not pleased with burnt offering. My sacrifice, O God, is a broken spirit; a broken and contrite heart you, God, will not despise." (*also look up 1 Sam 15:22, 2 Kings 22:19, Psalm 34:18 and Joel 2:13*) Joel 2:13 says, "Don't tear your clothing in your grief, but tear your hearts instead. Return to the LORD your God, for he is merciful and compassionate, slow to get angry and filled with unfailing love. He is eager to relent and not punish."

We now have to swing this toward the point I'm trying to make. Since we've established that God is always just trying to give us His best, the only thing that prevents that is us. We hold back, we limit our offering to Him. We only open the door just enough to give what we want to give, then wonder why God doesn't slip us His best through that tiny crack. If we leave the chain on the door, the pizza guy can't hand us the pizza! (*unless he tips the box sideways*) It's not a thing where God says, "HEY you're only giving me a little bit, so here I'm only giving you a little bit back!" God doesn't give to us as an act of economy, *'you get what you pay for.'* He gives to us according to His unfailing love and our willingness to receive. The door is our choice to limit what we receive. Jesus wants to come all the way in and bring all the blessings He has to give us. Sadly, we open the door only part way, to slip stuff out to Jesus, our limited offering.

"Here Lord, I will give you this much. Don't ask for more!" *SLAM*

We think He is holding His hands out to take from us, when He is really just asking us to let Him hold what we have, so He can give us WHAT HE HAS!!! <u>We have the need, He has the supply</u>. The trouble is that we try to supply for ourselves and we get greedy with what we acquire in our own strength. God can have a little of my candy, but not too much. I worked too hard to get it. God is saying all throughout scripture, *'I don't want your candy, I don't need your candy, I have something better and I want to give it to you!'*

<u>Limiting our offering means we limit our availability to God and we limit what He can give us.</u>

God wants to give to us, not get from us. In order for us to receive, we have to approach Him (*since He already extended the invitation from the cross*), laying down everything that will <u>get in the way</u> of Him giving us His all, His best. Empty hands can hold more than ones already full...

EMPTY HANDS CAN HOLD MORE THAN ONES ALREADY FULL!

Open the door. Take the chain off. Push the door all the way open. Empty your hands, empty your heart and just give Him full access (*a full offering*), because He has a heaven-sized moving truck parked just outside and He wants to bring it all in. Everything that He has, He wants to give you!

Moses wasn't always... Moses

I was telling a friend about the struggle my wife and I have with finding God's will sometimes. We want to honor God and give him exactly what He wants from us and through us. We pray. We ask. It's like we keep calling and leaving messages but He usually doesn't call us back. **OK, God never calls us back!** He usually just sort of confirms things along the way through the blessings we see in hindsight. So we do a lot of praying, waiting and guessing. We also do serious second-guessing. That sort of, 'maybe God wants us to not do this thing because' or 'maybe God didn't open this door because' stuff. We recently arrived in town and spent the night in our car at Wal-Mart. (*Not completely unusual for us*) It wasn't too bad and it wasn't too great either. We went to church the next morning to greet friends we hadn't seen in months. While relating our story, a friend was deeply saddened by the Wal-Mart thing.

I get it, our friend loves us and places honor on us. The idea of us being in need and uncomfortable, hurt his heart. So he and his family opened their home to us. We went to their house later that day and as we were settling in, he asked me why we didn't ask someone for a place to stay before then. I tried to explain that my wife and I are trying not to **'fix our way out of situations that God may have asked us to go into'**. (*I hope you understand that*)

You see, Millie and I want our faith to be real faith and not just theoretical. There should actually be steps, no LEAPS, into the unknown. It can be scary with no answers and no provision other than the character of God, but our decisions and actions should at least be available to that, if our faith is real. That is what I told my friend. He lovingly said, "but you're not Moses". I said "true, but don't you think God is still looking for more Moses?" He agreed. I told Him that if God was offering us the opportunity to be more 'Mosesy', then we wanted to say yes to it. My friend, who is himself a lot more like Moses than he knows, understood.

The next day, I was thinking about the conversation and the thought came to me, 'Moses wasn't always Moses'. It actually took 80 years for Moses to become the Moses we think of at the mention of his name. The combination of 40 years as a privileged brat and 40 years as a dirty unassuming working-guy, gave him the experiences he needed to become our Moses.

Moses, the servant of God and the deliverer of God's people!

Don't solve every problem. Don't fix every situation, until you know that's what God wants you to do. You may end up robbing yourself or others, of the very experiences that God intend to use, to make you a Moses!

Crayon Jesus

A recent VBS camp was about being made in the image of a creative God. As I was considering the lessons for camp, I wanted to include a special project that had been rolling around in my head for several months. Last winter I frequented a Red Robin burger place and had admired some wall art they had up. One piece was a cartoon face made out of crayons. The crayons were laid down and stacked on top of each other and all you could see was the very ends, like pixels. It looked very cool and I knew I wanted to make a picture of Jesus like that.

Each of the first 3 nights, I would have the kids come into the teaching room where I was and I would be doing a little something on that particular project. The first night, as the kids came in, I was pulling crayons out of boxes and just laying them in the frame, which was in an easel like position. There was no pattern at this point. All the colors were randomly in there. When the kids all sat down and got quiet, I told them this is a project for the 4th night, but it is going to take a while to finish, so I was starting it now. I explained that I had a plan for my masterpiece and the first step was putting everything inside the box frame, just like putting all the right ingredients from a great recipe, into a bowl. Then I laid the frame down and moved on to the lesson for that night.

The second night when they came in, the box was nearly full of crayons, though still unsorted. I showed them the tweezers I was going to use to move individual crayons around once it was full, then I put it aside and started the lesson for night two.

The third night, the box frame was laying flat on the table and I demonstrated pulling one crayon at a time out with the tweezers and replacing it with a different color. I told the kids that all the right pieces were in the box. I just had to take the time to move each to the right place to finish my masterpiece. Then I moved on to the lesson for the third night.

The last night of camp, as the kids came in, the box frame was laid down on a table, front and center. It was a bit above the heads of the kids so they couldn't see what it looked like yet. I got their attention and they quieted down. I pulled out another crayon and mumbled just loud enough for them to hear me, "that doesn't go there," and as I replaced it with another one, "this one does!" Then I looked up and announced, "It's finished. My masterpiece is done!"

Before I revealed the final picture to the kids, I asked them why I was moving them one at a time instead of a handful at a time? They said that even though a handful would seem faster, maybe if I tried to move too much all at one time, the rest would get jumbled up too. I agreed and said that when God is working on the masterpiece inside each us, He knows that we get jumbled up inside too, if we have to change too much all at once. So, in the same way, He takes the time to adjust us one piece, one idea at a time. I then asked the kids if they were ready to see my masterpiece. They yelled out 'YES' and I showed them.
(*It's on the back cover of this book*)

4,316 crayons, all rearranged according to an imagined design! They all asked if they could come touch it. So, they lined up and came to the stage. As they touched it, they smiled at me like they couldn't believe that all these crayons were moved into place to make my picture. They sat down and we finished the lesson...

God planned us, from the beginning, as masterpieces with a WOW-factor of a billion!!!

The issue is if we are going to let Him rearrange our crayons or not. Do we face each day saying in our hearts, "Go ahead Lord, grab the tweezers and change whatever you want to change in me" or do we ask God to fit into our plans for the day and tell Him, "You know how I am, that's just how it is."

The first step to becoming a masterpiece is yielding, surrendering to God. We need to believe in His compelling desire to transform us into something so much more fantastic than we could ever have imagined for ourselves.

We also need to believe in the (*often secret*) process He has to use to get us there. Because there are no surprises to God, no "Plan B", no "Oops, I gotta make an adjustment now". He already knew all our decisions (*past, present and future*) and factored them into His plan to transform us. His plan! It's only a secret to us. We just have to believe and yield.

Don't fear the tweezers and I'll see you on the easel!

My BIGGEST fish

So, I was in the middle of a *Face book* group conversation. I don't remember the details, only that at one point, a comment was made, "bigger fish". It was made because someone thought another comment was trivial. Thus the abbreviated use of "there are bigger fish to fry", meaning there are more important things that we could have been discussing (*which was true*), but the moment that I read that comment, a thought popped into my mind. "Lord, help me find my BIGGEST fish!" (*That greatest THING you want me to do*) "Lord, just tell me what you want me to do and I will do it." Because, we all know there is a greatest THING He made us for, right? Some event, some missions trip, some new ministry, some place or time when we jump in and save the day? Don't you feel that way too?? Well, honestly that's how I have thought for quite a while. "Lord, what is that one thing, that BIGGEST fish that you have for me to do? I want to do it and not waste both of our times on smaller issues anymore. I want to get to it... c'mon Lord, let's get going!"
(*That would be me, obviously, mistaken*)
So, this season that Millie and I are in was not in our plans at all. It is a sort of forced humility time. A great big God trick. An epic 'bait-n-switch'! Meaning, we are doing things that are 'uncomfortable', for basically no money, for strangers. We're isolated, restricted and our living quarters smell like a backed up septic tank! BUT, in this season, separated from all the comfort we knew, God has our attention! He is refocusing us on a different image of what walking with Him is supposed to look like. We are supposed to look, talk and live like Jesus <u>not like Christians</u>. Yes, sadly there's often a very big difference.

My favorite verse in the Bible is Micah 6:8, "...do justly, love mercy and walk humbly with your God." It's God saying that these 3 things are the way we are supposed to live. They are heart requirements! Everything we think, do and say should be made from this simple recipe. I love how this verse simplifies all those laws and the *'thou shalt nots'*. It boils them right down to a tiny cookie.

Back to my biggest fish -

In this season, God has been doing a lot of , "Hey Russ, what do you think about this?" kind of things. So, He has asked me, "What if your biggest fish isn't a THING, isn't an EVENT? What if your biggest fish is just BEING LIKE ME?" BOOM, right between the eyes!!!
Could our greatest calling from God be to just be an extraordinary person, in our ordinary lives? Do justly, love mercy and walk humbly. On Tuesdays, do justly. At work, love mercy. Walk humbly with God as we're driving to the store, with our neighbors, with our paycheck and home, with our talents and with our time??? Seems obvious right? Except when you grow up thinking 'being a Christian' is about events and programs and getting people to come to your church or missions trips to those poor places or collecting Inspirational books or going to conferences or the latest praise CD or handing out tracts or correcting the 'heathen' or (*I think you get it*). Are those things wrong? Not necessarily. But are they FAITH in action or are they ABOUT faith? <u>Are they how Jesus lived, or are they what Christians do</u>? (*Sometimes those are different things, even though our intentions might be good*)
Could 'how I am' be more valuable to God than 'what I do'? I guess that might explain why there are plenty of times when I don't know <u>what I'm supposed to do</u>, but the bible is pretty clear on <u>how I'm supposed to be</u>. Micah 6:8 (*and a few hundred other verses*). If this is all true, then **I** am the diamond in the rough, the buried treasure, the biggest fish of my life! ME
"Get the pan out Lord, I believe that I'm ready to be fried."

Don't be surprised if God invites you to some huge DO's,
while you're working out HOW to be.

Swiss army Jesus

There's a reason that the Greeks, Norse and Romans had so many gods and it's not because it makes for cool action movies. The human mind (*without God's influence*) is incapable of imagining all the character traits and powers of God, in one being.

ALL RIGHTEOUSNESS and ALL FORGIVENESS in the same person, can that even work!

"Look fellow Vikings, we need a god for fighting and a different god for affection. Hey, let's have a god for storms and a god for raisin toast!!!"

Long ago, around 1884, some folks came up with a Swiss Army pocketknife or as we also call it, a multi-tool. It has a long sharp blade, a couple screwdrivers, stuff for sewing, picking your teeth, opening cans and bottles, taking the scales off fish and a bunch of other things. It's amazing and so versatile. Once you get used to having a multi-tool, you lean on it all the time. It becomes your 'go-to' piece of equipment for all your needs.
What's the point?

Humanity often finds it hard to understand a God who's over everything, but we can picture a god who feels and acts like us. I like being tough and manly and mean, so I am going to honor the god I just made in my own image. "HAIL MARS, GOD OF WAR!!!" (*or maybe*) I can't stand people picking on me just because they are bigger and stronger than I am, so I worship you goddess of wisdom, because my brain is more important than their muscles, "HAIL ATHENA!"
Cultures always want a god that makes them feel 'right', the way they are. I don't have to change because the god I picked already agrees with me. Sadly, just because you

pick a god that says you're right, doesn't mean that you ARE right! God declared Himself through Jesus to be all righteous and all kind. He was showing us that He is the God of everything. The only God, the true God, a paradox of every wonderful thing that we can't be all at once! He is 'The Impossible' and that is why He's God and why we need Him for every situation.

I will not offer my allegiance to a god who is made in my own image, for I have met myself.

I really do need a Swiss Army God that covers every single issue of life. It's funny, but my Jesus journey began with looking for an all-in-one God. I had gotten saved a few years earlier, but then I had a season of living in my appetites and found myself shipwrecked on my own decisions. Hating all that I had become, I went to find a church that would answer my life (*because life is a question that needs to be answered*). Every church I went to told me one main point. Either it was that I suck and should burn in hell or Jesus loves me so much. Each church leaned on one of those 2 incompatible ideas. But my heart knew that I needed to find a church that raised both truths together. I am completely unlovable and completely loved at the same time. I had no peace in my heart until I found a church like that. My innermost being knew I needed a God over my everything.

We all need a God we can lean on all the time. In the good and in the bad. When we're likeable and when we're not.

Kind of a Swiss Army Jesus

Boldly
(quite honestly, I struggle very deeply with this issue myself)

I have written and spoken on this idea many times before. That's not to say that I am an expert or have anything to offer that is special on the subject. It's more of a recurring theme! It would seem that God is repeating Himself to me because I am thickheaded on the subject. The seed thought for this came from staring at a deli counter ticket.
                    Number 49!

I find that I often expect a waiting list to see God or at least a series of obligations to fulfill. The idea that I am always at the head of the line *(ticket number 1)*, is a difficult thought for me to reconcile.
In Hebrews 4:16, we are told, '*Let us therefore come boldly to the throne of grace, that we may obtain mercy and find grace to help in time of need.*'
        There are things we love about this verse, like the throne of grace, and the mercy and help it offers. The part we struggle with, is the 'come boldly'. How can we push open the Throne room door and just strut in? How dare we!? Yet, that is Paul's instruction to us, 'come boldly'!
        Boldly is defined like this: <u>not hesitating</u> or fearful in the face of actual or possible danger or <u>rebuff</u>; courageous and daring: not hesitating to break the rules of <u>propriety</u>; forward; <u>impudent</u>.
        Seriously, look up those underlined words and chew on that a bit!!! How can Paul tell us to disrespect the holiness of God like this? It hurts my heart in a way, to think that I can put aside everything I know about my sinful self, all of my <u>well deserved shame</u> and say "so what".

But here we go -
        Just before it, in verse 15, it says 'For we do not have a High Priest who cannot sympathize with our weaknesses, but was in all *points* tempted as *we are, yet* without sin.'

THAT is the verse before the 'THEREFORE COME BOLDLY TO THE THRONE' verse!!! Come with me a little deeper into my scripture madness for just a minute more.

The '*therefore*' in verse 16 is saying to us, because of verse 15, we can do/believe what verse 16 says. Because Jesus understands us, but didn't sin, we should come boldly.

Bold is defined as: *Assured, Confident, Adventurous*...
FREE!

Come to God's throne, His **place of ultimate power and authority**, boldly. **Be** bold... be **FREE to walk in**to God's most protected and holy of areas **and ask for what you want!** He is your gracious father and He actually waits for you to barge in and say, "Hey Dad, can you help me with something please?"

Yes, we all struggle with the 'be free' part. We feel like there should be some hesitation or at least some humility in the face of our sinfulness. But verse 15 says He went through the exact same temptations that we do. He understands and He sympathizes with us! His arms are not folded as if to say, "*if you must come in, fine, but I know how bad you are on the inside!*" We approach a throne that is appeased. The debt is paid, there isn't supposed to be any shame! IT'S PAID FOR - **Come because you are free, free from shame!!!**

Ok, so the previous words in the bold font,
   let me just paste them together here again.
Come to God's place of ultimate power and authority.
      Be FREE to walk in and ask for what you want!
            Come because you are free from shame!!!

...and that is just too wonderful of a truth, for the devil to let us believe it UNCHALLENGED!

So guard your heart on this one, because it's true!!!!!

No es como yo

I do not speak Spanish! I am not very good at languages in general and even though my wife of nearly twelve years is Puerto Rican, I have struggled to capture even a few of her words.

She has however, introduced me to a lot of Spanish culture, from food and traditions, to worship music. I have several favorite foods and traditions that I have made a part of my own personal culture.

There is a song called, "No es como yo" by Jesus Adrian Romero. In English it means 'YOU are not like me'. I have read and liked the translation for the lyrics of the song, but it is the title that really stirs my heart. This man is saying that he follows God because <u>God is not like him</u>.

He loves God because God is not like him.
He trusts God because God is not like him.
He rests in God because God is not like him.
He is safe with God because God is not like him.

I can connect deeply with this idea, "God, you are not like me".

I thank God that He is not like me. I have met me and I have seen the ungodly things that I think and do. I couldn't love a God like me. I couldn't trust or feel safe with a God like me. I couldn't rely on a promise from a God like me. I couldn't tell those I love to hope in a God like me.

It is His willingness to look at me with love in His eyes, that draws me to Him. It is His willingness to prove that He is better than I deserve, yet willing to be completely faithful to me, that draws me to Him. It is this vast portfolio of beauty and math smashed together, that we call creation, that takes my breath away and draws me to Him. It is the history of broken mankind being chased by a gentle and forgiving God, that draws me to Him.

It is because He is not like me!

Kick the can

There's an episode of the Twilight Zone from 1962, called *'Kick the can'*. The story takes place completely in and around an assisted living facility for older folks who've been forgotten. The residents all have various health issues, but nothing too serious. Their biggest problem seems to be boredom, life has past them by and there are no more trains coming!

I have recently become more acquainted with the lifestyle of older people (*since I am almost there myself*) and have noticed that the lack of purpose seems to drain their vigor faster than the achy bones do. I guess spiritually speaking it's the '*hope*' that really drains out of them. I believe a lot of elderly people thought their later years would be the reward for all their labors, all their service and even, all their financial savings, though that is rarely the case. Even in those occasional cases when someone gets to retirement with their health and finances intact, they often waste those resources on trying to make up for lost time, reliving their imagined 'glory-days' or hiding themselves away from the rest of the world in a well planned cocoon.

Back to the kick the can episode, there's one guy who feels like there should be a way to rekindle the fire in his life, regain his hope and purpose. It occurs to him that perhaps the disconnect he feels is from the giving up of children's games. If that's the case, then perhaps it could also be the reconnect. So he tries to talk the other residents into playing kick the can with him in hopes that it will magically restore their youth. The part of the story that always makes me cry is his desperate plea to his disbelieving friends, **"I can't play kick the can alone!"** Well, of course they join him, regain their youth, escape their lonely ending and go running off into the woods as kids again.

I think that episode has a lot of good heart in it. We weren't created to spend our first 70 years gathering, so we can lock ourselves in our rooms and feast by ourselves. That is a wasted life. I think our years are meant to live and not be caught up in preparing for a season decades later that we simply are not promised. I realize some of you reading are thinking about 'being good stewards financially' and to be honest, I struggle with what things are most important to be good stewards of. Is it finances or time or talents or love or family or home or (*perhaps*) those around us? Life and people may be a more important thing to be good stewards of. In the Bible, people asked Jesus, 'who are my neighbors?' In response, we got the story of the Good Samaritan! Jesus also said that the two commandments that are important are love God with all that you are and love your neighbor as yourself. Maybe what we are supposed to do for all our years is gather love from God and give love to others? I think there is a lot to the idea of reconnecting with simpler things, a more pure faith and sharing life together.

You can't just give stuff away, can you? You can't just go out there and make things better, can you? Can you just go help and live like the words of Jesus are true? The teachings of Jesus are either just lovely metaphors or they are dead-on truth!
once more...
The teachings of Jesus are either just lovely metaphors or they are dead-on truth!

Nobody can play kick the can alone. Nobody can really live in a financially well-planned and nicely decorated coffin. That's just called waiting to die. We have to continue to leap in faith even if we need a walker to do it! Pray, serve, give, laugh, help and hug. In fact, hug everyone you can!

Do it all in the name of Jesus until your time is up. Remember, <u>Jesus' earthly ministry didn't end until the hour He died.</u> **Heaven** was His retirement.

Out-living your own story

I was watching a movie about an older gentleman who was writing down all the stories of his younger days. He was telling about how great his adventures were and then sadly commented on the fact that everyone else on those pages was dead. He had out-lived his own story. His voice was full of sadness and he looked out in the distance complaining quietly about still being alive.

It made me think about how we are tricked by the world and the devil, into accepting that same fate for ourselves. In Gen 5:24 it says, "*Enoch walked faithfully with God; then he was no more, because God took him away.*"

That is the plan God has for us, walk with Him (*keep walking... still walking with Him*) and He brings us home. He never intended for us to have a few decades of sitting around, telling old stories and waiting to die! John 10:10 says an <u>abundant life</u>, not a life that slowly runs out and then we wait to die. The devil is a liar, this world is a liar and quite honestly, our own bodies are liars. If our strength comes from Him, our hope comes from Him and our purpose comes from Him, then either we do believe in God and walk with Him until He takes us home or we are believing the lies and give up. *Give up?* Heck, we will start making a well organized list of reasons why we can't, shouldn't and won't go on with God as we get older.

"*I did my share...*
I did more than others...
I met the requirements...
I don't have anymore to give...
I've gotten hurt by the church...
I've earned my rest...
That's for younger people to do...
That's not my thing..."

If our strength comes from Him, our hope comes from Him and our purpose comes from Him, then we don't need the source of our strength and motivation to be our own aging bodies and minds.

If our strength comes from Him, our hope comes from Him and our purpose comes from Him, then we don't need the source to be natural.

If our strength comes from Him, our hope comes from Him and our purpose comes from Him, then what shall we say to all of those excuses? *"Sorry, I can STILL do all things through Christ who strengthens me!!! So there"* -

I refuse to outlive my own story. When life changes my situations, I may need to make new friends and find new ways to serve, but I will because God is with me. When my wife dies and my heart is broken, I will not throw my hands in the air and say I have given enough, I will remember that it was always God giving through me and I will let Him do it again. If I find myself in a wheelchair or unable to see, my story will not end, my usefulness will not end, my serving and walking with God will not end, because my story isn't over until He walks me home!

I think the secret is in the planning, the commitment and the resolution that God isn't finished with me until the very last page. Plan to be flexible, commit to adapt and change and grow. Decide right now and here, that your father is the KING OF KINGS AND THE GOD OF ALL CREATION AND HE WILL NOT CAST YOU ASIDE BECAUSE OF YOUR AGE OR SITUATION, YOU ARE HIS BELOVED CHILD!

'Made in His image' should mean something.

It should mean that **nothing natural can count me out** -

Polarized lens

I have this thing called a polarized lens. It goes on the front of a camera and changes the way you see things. Being polarized allows it to 'sift' light waves to block out reflections. You know, on a really sunny day, when you look at the window of a car or at a lake or pond? You try to see into it or through it, but there's a reflection. We also call this glare.

It makes it hard to see what's underneath.

When we can see what's really in the water, we can see the rocks and plants and even the fish that are ALWAYS THERE, we just couldn't see them before. The reflection or glare blocked our view. The filter doesn't help us see better, it helps us see more clearly! It helps us see what's **really there**, hiding under the surface.

We're supposed to let Jesus be like a polarized lens for how we see the Bible. Getting to know **Him** will help us see **what's really in there!** The Bible will become clear with a Jesus filter. We'll hear things more the way Jesus would say them. We'll understand that a God who loved us and saved us and forgave us, isn't all of a sudden going to be mean and a bully, now that we're His kids! It's like the Bible teaches us God's words and Jesus teaches us God's voice. (*we need both*)

So when you read the Bible, you can think about how Jesus would say it. THAT'S how we start to think like Him! Philippians 2:5 says, "Let this mind be in you, that was also in Christ Jesus."

Not only will we see the Bible more clearly, but looking at others 'through Jesus' will help us see them more clearly too. Remember that bully at school or at work? We will see more than his anger, we will see the reasons why he is mean to others, what is broken in his heart. This will help us to treat him the way Jesus would, with compassion. It will help us to understand that his words and actions toward us don't need to sting or define us. Because we can now see ourselves through the eyes of Jesus as well!

We will see that we are the greatly loved, child of the living God -

JESUS - He's like a pair of polarized glasses for our heart!

Racist by design

I was recently discussing racism with a teenager. The subject has become a trigger word for violent conflicts, social outcry, political retaliation, public disgrace, embarrassingly poor communication and divisive labeling between human beings. This young friend, who is very intelligent, was picking out comments others make and labeling them as racist. Putting a <u>stain of judgment on them,</u> for judging others. This friend also said she would not date a white guy. (*Seeing the problem here?*)

So let me try to redefine the issue of racist, as I did with her. I told her that her comment about '*white guys*' was racist but that it's ok because we're all racist to some degree and that it was normal. She took some offense to my statements, so I asked her to allow me to explain. I told her that the way our brains work is by gathering information and filing it. Our eyes, ears, hands and noses are some of our gathering stations. Our experiences also add information that we sort and file to make up our understanding of the world. When we are a little kid and the boy with red hair is mean to us, it goes into our file system. Red head is mean. The next time a red headed kid is mean to us, another paper goes into our mental file cabinet. The third time, we see a pattern and we may decide to build a new file called <u>red heads are all mean</u>. IS that correct? No not really, but it's all the info we have on redheads, so it IS CORRECT ACCORDING TO OUR LIMITED DATA. Does that make us a racist? No, but it will make us suspicious of redheads.

- *Suspicious of redheads?*
In today's world that would make us racist -

If we decide that all redheads are evil and we seal that file as '**fact**', we may never be willing to open it up for new information or a possible change of opinion. That would make us wrong! That also makes us racist and a normal human being. We actually like sealed files more than ones that we have to keep open and adjust our opinions of. It's easier to just say, "ALL Cadillac drivers are snobs" than to hope there are nice ones out there. A sealed opinion file is a lot less work. We just glance at the front of the folder, 'People from India smell funny' and the conversation is done just like that. No discussion, no change, I'm right and you're wrong.

If someone lives with unsealed files, it requires continual reevaluation and constant sorting. There is no folder stamped *'All of those type of people are bad'*. It makes us see individuals and not categories. We also get hurt more with open files. Giving people the chance to prove us wrong or prove us right. If we label and judge them, we never get disappointed. Mostly because we've already decided that we're only going to acknowledge our own opinion.

In the Garden of Eden, Adam and Eve were getting their information (*their judgments*) from God. God walked with them and told them what was good and what was evil, until they decided they wanted to make their own judgments and build their own files. Going from accepting the assessments of an all-knowing, all-seeing God to judging by our limited perception, leaves us with completely flawed and utterly selfish opinions, in place of truth.

Racism is simply one way we judge.

We lump information together just to make it easier on us. As we quickly file them into folders, we tend to forget that these are all people, created by God, made in His image, deserving of respect, love and having a voice.

It is simply human nature to make decisions in our own strength. It's wrong but it's normal. The problem is what you do with this natural tendency. Do you let it lead you or do you tell it to *'hold on a second, let's see how you line up with God's word before I believe you'*?

Now that I am 'enlightened' or 'woke', shall I label others as racists and belittle them for it?

I can't see taking a stand against another person's poor judgment, by standing on my own poor judgment to do it.

*One of my favorite movies is the 1957 version of **12 Angry Men**. It's all about being prejudice on a lot of different levels, for a lot of different reasons. Expecting the worst from people based on one of their personal adjectives, instead of seeing the actual individual. Worth the watching!*

Hand sanitizer

We use hand sanitizer to kill harmful germs that we pick up from touching stuff. I myself often use sanitizer when I've been with a bunch of kids or coughing people. It has become **'an accepted safety routine'**. There's one big problem with that, the hand sanitizer is actually absorbing into our skin. The chemicals that are strong enough to kill 99% of germs also happen to be very bad for our health. The skin is the largest organ of the human body and it absorbs these chemicals. They can cause hormone disruptions and weaken the immune system. So by grabbing a quick fix for the germ problem, we may be slowly poisoning our bodies.

Over-reaction is something we humans do in many areas. We're experts at it! People sometimes see one issue that upsets them and react to that problem with such narrow focus that they create more problems. We have created economic, environmental, ecological and social problems of gigantic sizes, in response to a smaller problem. One example is when beetles in Australia started eating the Sugarcane crops. Someone brought in Cane Toads from Hawaii to eat the beetles, but other animals started dying, because the Cane Toads are poisonous. By reacting to one problem without looking at the bigger picture or researching the consequences, a much bigger problem was created.

We do this spiritually too.

Even entire churches and denominations choose to embrace a change or strategy to 'fix' a problem or 'deal with' an issue, while not seeing the other problems the change will allow into the congregation. But, let's focus on us as individuals.

- If I get involved with a church and I feel neglected, embarrassed or lied to, I may decide that all churches are bad and never go to one again. Then I will have traded an awkward personal situation, for permanently putting a wall between God and myself.

- If I volunteer, but don't get recognized for all my efforts, I may decide not to help ever again. Then I will have traded a chance to humbly make the world a bit brighter, for closing myself up from new friendships built on giving hope.

- If GOD does something, or allows something, that I don't want or understand, I may decide that the Bible isn't true! Then I will have traded my ego (*a person's sense of self-esteem or self-importance*) for my faith!

I know it's hard to work through problems and awkward, embarrassing situations, but it's what we're supposed to do, to get to the other side of them. '*Hand sanitizer*' is a quick decision to deal with the feelings and not the cause of the feelings. I understand that it's easier and faster. Life just takes so much effort sometimes that we want the easy way, but 'the easy way' might just be spiritual poison! The Bible says to <u>stand</u> wearing the belt of truth in Ephesians 6:14.

God never says, "<u>jump</u> to conclusions" or "<u>rush</u> to judgment"!

Jesus never adjusted the truth to make His journey easier.

He ate with dirty people and they saw the love of God in Him. He walked with sinners and they saw forgiveness. He bore the cross and never once reached for the quick fix. We were far too important to Him!

Rescue party

Rescue Party: a group of people who attempt to rescue, find or save a person or people in danger, especially a person lost while mountain climbing, in a jungle or somewhere at sea; to free or deliver from any confinement, violence, danger or evil; to liberate from actual restraint; to remove or withdraw from a state of exposure to evil; to rescue a prisoner from the enemy.

For what I'm talking about here, we will use a slight combination of the first and last definitions.
   "A group of people who attempt to rescue a prisoner from the enemy."

We all agree that if someone is in terrible danger, they need a rescue party? Even if they caused the danger to themselves, they need rescuing. If they don't know that they are in terrible danger, they still need a rescue party.

Here is the simple breakdown of how life is and what God wants from us: the secret to our purpose here on earth.

We are all either in need of rescuing or, having been rescued, are now asked to be a part of the rescue party. There it is all summed up. The secret of life! Rescued or searching for the lost. Consider Jesus and the disciples. He came to rescue them because they were on the path to perishing. He rescued them, then immediately started to show them how to rescue others. The journeys they went on? Rescue missions. The books of the Bible they wrote? Invitations to be rescued and instructions on how to rescue others.
   From the moment the clock started ticking, we are all adrift doing the doggy paddle waiting to die. The 'Jesus-ship' comes along side asking us to reach out and be rescued. If we say yes to God's offer, then we board the ship and join the

mission. There's no time to drop us off at the pier so we can stroll into the coffee shop and make our plans to build an empire for ourselves. Those who claim to love God but live like that are living in complete contradiction to the life and teaching of Jesus.

Truth isn't something we create or change, we can only accept it or pretend it's not real. **Truth doesn't need us to agree with it to make it right**. Jesus came to seek and save those who are lost! (*Luke 19:10*) After that, He tells those with Him, "*I have set you an example so that you should do as I have done for you.*" (*John 13:15*)

There it is. Just be like Jesus. That's enough.

But don't forget, the devil is called the father of lies for a reason. One of his best lies is that we have to get ready to help rescue others. You know, 4 years of Bible school, 6 years experience leading small groups, 2 years on the board of some committee and a bunch of other '*godly-distractions*'. Jesus told us to reach out our hand toward others, just as He did for us.

That's it. You're ready!

Problem proximity

My wife and I were visiting a church in a different town and the Pastor was speaking on encouraging and exhortation. He said that we, too often, feel free to correct others and get in their space about it, while avoiding drawing close enough to really encourage them as well. I have to agree with that estimation of our human condition, mine included. (*Though I am sad to admit it*)

He went on to say that we need to "earn that kind of privilege in the lives of others". He was saying that people are more likely to respond to the wise council of someone who's invested love or compassion in their life and in their journey. It's what I call <u>Problem Proximity</u>.

You may not know that I attended a Bible College in the 80's, or that this particular school was very big on doctrine and the laws of God, but a bit less enthusiastic about real mercy and the tenderness of God's heart for all of His broken children. That was my experience and my interpretation. I know others who found the fullness of God there, so I apologize for my seemingly harsh words. What I did learn there was a clear understanding that the Word of God is infallible. I got a lot of Bible knowledge in school but it wasn't until years later that I started to really get the wisdom of how to live it and not just quote it.

I think this 'problem proximity' thing is the key to real fruit in relationships of all kinds. If I have sat with you as you grieved. If I have bailed the boat with you during your storms and if I have put my cloak over your wounds to protect your dignity and your life, then my voice will be one of love and comfort. It will sound like love, even if I tell you that you are wrong. You will have seen proof that I am for you and not against you. There will be an abundance of love-credit in the account of my testimony and you will give my motives the benefit of the doubt.

My Jesus has done this in my life and because of it, I have never heard His correction as "I told you so" or "I'm

117

right, you're wrong." His corrections reach my heart as words pleading for my safety, pleading for my conscience and pleading for my future. The 'thou-shalt-nots' are gentle wisdom from a better vantage point to keep me from well-laid traps. They are never limitations from a bully who holds all the cards. He is my King, my savior, my friend, my love and His words are all good. His investment in my wellbeing and His *'proximity in my problems'* have both earned my trust and my heart's passion. I think that is the point of relationship anyway! I see similarities in the words of Jesus in Mt 25:31-45, where even the Lord says that <u>our investment in those that He loves</u>, is an important requirement in our relationship with Him. An act of love from us toward others is a just reaction to the many acts of love from Him toward us.

Perhaps that is the main place the church has gone wrong in the past? We've earned the reputation of an elite group unwilling to help the sinner get up and dust them off, but so committed to pointing at them when they've fallen down and happily proclaiming their filth. Maybe that's not you but it has been the church around the world far too often. Then we wonder why the truth of God has no bearing in their dirty lives. We have stripped it of its comfort and denied its desire to be a companion and help to the fallen. Instead, we make it an embarrassing scarlet letter of shame. An un-invested bully and not the friend who is closer than a brother (*Prov 18:24*), who was born to sit beside them in their troubles (*Prov 17:17*) and walk them to a better situation. A better them!

"A misled heart is more often drawn away from sin, not by the preaching from pulpits, but by the Godly council of one who has had a gentle proximity to their previous problems!"

Scary neighborhoods

This one is about a grown-up topic, but I will try to keep it in the 'G' format.

A couple of months ago, I decided to watch an independent documentary about a community that is exclusively for people with criminal records. It is located *'out there'* in the real world, right next to everyone else, but it is only for folks with, as I said, a criminal record. Ok, a specific criminal record. Adults who have hurt children!

Not a topic I am comfortable with. I have spent 30 plus years trying to bring hope and healing through Jesus, to kids. I have no fondness for people with that particular sin in their stories. Look I'm going to be honest for this, because Jesus deals with our honesty, very kindly and very faithfully, so we can walk through my struggle together as a sort of fieldtrip.

If it were up to me, I would rank sins on a scale of 1 to 10 with jaywalking being number 1 and hurting children being an 85!!!!! But God sees 'broken a little' and 'broken a lot' as just broken. It's probably how He can be so kind to everyone. This journey is about Him asking me to see what He sees, however, this journey will have God taking me into some scary neighborhoods.

This documentary was very honest and so were those interviewed. Nobody made any excuses or condoned what they had done. If anything, the remorse for their crimes weighed so heavily on most of them that it was a daily struggle to face their own existence. It was so real and so sad, that by the end, I only saw broken people.

I didn't feel hate or disgust. I only saw broken people that God wants to set free because He loves them and because only His love can stop the cycle of broken people, breaking others! I think God loves dealing with uncomfortable areas in my heart and mind. That is the only explanation for my next thought. "God? Do you want me to go tell them that you love them?"

(*Deep breath...*) Seriously? Yes I told God that if He wants me to tell them that He forgives them and He loves them too, that I would do it.

Now, before you think well of me and say nice things about me and all that, please know that I wasn't happy asking God that question. I was a bit ticked-off! I was very uncomfortable with the thought and hoping He would immediately come back with, "ARE YOU NUTS? Of course not!"

In my universe, when God doesn't answer me, it's like He's suggesting, "well, Russ, I think you already know the answer don't you?"

When I ask, "God, am I supposed to share your HOLY and PURE message of love with that UNCLEAN CHILD ABUSER Karen, WHO I THINK DESERVES NO PITY AT ALL?"

God says, "Are you asking me if I love Karen?"
"No Lord, I'm asking if this unclean child abuser Karen is worthy of..."

"Russ, do I love Karen?"
"Lord, wait... I'm asking if..."

"Russ do I love Karen?" (*sigh and tears*)
"Of course you do my gentle and wise King. You love all of us!"

So I get no credit for being a better man. God gets the credit for allowing me to know Him on my own terms at first and then drawing me closer to His terms and His image. He also gets the credit for taking me into places that I used to think were scary neighborhoods, which are really just places of shadow, in need of His light!

I will visit these broken people and offer them hugs and a nonjudgmental ear in the name of my loving Jesus who was also known as "a friend of sinners."

Riding their bus

This is one of my oldest and dearest personal truths. I've used it every week of my life for decades. It comes up in my head and heart in lots of situations and I think God has used it to make me a better Russ!

As with many great personal truths, it was borne from a lot of self-reflection with God and years of my own self-disappointment. If you watch mankind's common struggles, there are great lessons to be learned there. Usually they aren't lessons involving loud correction. They are lessons involving gentle understanding.

Someone lost in a cave doesn't need me to stand at the entrance and yell, "YOU'RE LOST, DO AS I SAY!" They need me to go in there, find them, calm them down and walk them out!

Isn't that what Jesus did?
>Left heaven, came to earth.
>Yielded perfection, took on mortal flesh.
>Abandoned eternity, lived one day at a time.
>Gave up all-knowledge, went to school like us.
>No longer safe, walked our filthy-broken paths.
>Postponed judging us, took the judgment upon
>>Himself.
>Chose the loneliness of separation from the Father,
>>so He could invite us to join Him in a new freedom!
>>THAT is riding OUR bus!

He let us know that He understood what we go through, NOT by saying. "I understand" but by kindly, gently and with great integrity, walking our path. We saw Him in our muck and mud! Let's admit that when we are burdened, the last thing we want to hear is, "Oh, I know exactly what you're going through", from someone standing on life's sidelines or sitting in the bleachers. This Jesus of mine dethroned Himself, <u>put on my trousers and shoes</u> and <u>carried every weight I would ever carry</u>. <u>Faced down every fear that would jump out at me</u>. My Jesus. My example.

So this riding their bus came about when I was doing a Jr. High Bible study. I noticed that the kids seemed to be like passengers in their own out-of-control lives. Like they were on a bus with their name on it and quite frequently it seemed they were sitting in the back, face pressed against the window as it went speeding along, mouthing the words, "I don't know where I'm going."
God had me picture it like this...
...Russ I need you to understand that these poor kids start as innocent bystanders, then suddenly a brawl begins. Who they think they are confronts who they think they want to be. Bad enough? Well, who their friends want them to be starts shoving who their parents and teachers tell them they are and could be. Who God really made them to be then jumps into the ring with all these others. This is just too much to sift through, don't you think? Oh, wait a minute. The hormones!!! How they 'feel' in the heat of the moment. That's some epic struggle they go through. As adults we usually correct them, "grow up" or "just be your self". They would probably love to do that, if they just knew how. This is not making excuses for them, just trying to understand what they face. <u>THIS IS THEIR BUS!</u>

(for some of us adults, this didn't end with the teen years. Hormones might get replaced by careers, worldly-expectations and fears. We can still be passengers on our own runaway bus)

Jesus, only Jesus, can show you how to ride someone's bus.

step 1 - getting on the bus
RUN ALONG SIDE someone's bus, but instead of yelling, "YOU'RE GOING THE WRONG WAY!!!", invest in them, play with them, love them and LISTEN TO THEM (*give*

their words and emotions importance, even if you don't agree) and they will let you on their bus at the next stop! There is no greater privilege than being invited into someone's personal 'out of control'.

It's important to know that you don't have to agree, just understand

   Understanding without agreement... *hssssssssssss, kachunk squeeeeeek...* the bus door opens.

step 2 - once you're on the bus
         The normal thing to do would be to get on the bus and say, "Hey... ummm, do you know your headed for the guardrail?" This would probably push the person to react with, "Ok, so get off the bus!" *(connection ended because you were trying to tell them how to drive, when they're sitting in the back - an emotional mile from the steering wheel)*
         Instead, sit beside them quietly and wait. Wait for the right moment to say, "I'm sorry it's like this for you." Then be quiet again. *(this is the part where you are in the cave calmly reassuring the lost hiker that you can be trusted)* A broken person needs to know you're with them, even if they hit the guardrail.

Understand that you don't have to run your own life into the guardrail with them
                    *...it's THEIR bus, not yours**

         Isn't that what Jesus did for us? And when we were ready, we asked Him to lead us off that bus and to let us join Him on His journey. WHEN WE WERE READY! There is a very wise verse I need to share right now.
         Jude 22-23 *"And of some have compassion, making a difference: And others save with fear, pulling them out of the fire; hating even the garment spotted by the flesh."*

Whether you're there when they ask for help getting off that bus, or you're there when it finally crashes, you have to be there, <u>riding their bus!</u>

Do you want to see God grow more of His son in you? Ride someone's bus. Listen to them, taste their story, feel their struggle and look for the spark of their flickering hope. Even if you end up disagreeing with all of it, they will stop being a '*them*' and turn into a David or a Susan. A real person!

Mobs and crowds are a different story. They are a construct of the devil to imitate God's view of community. But, if we could pull someone from the mob and convince them to let us ride their personal bus, that changes everything. Even if it's just for that one person. Isn't that your story with Jesus anyways?

Weren't we all saved as individuals from one crowd or another? It happened when we found out that Jesus cared enough to ride our personal bus?

Simple compassion can change conflict into communication and understanding.

Compassion unties the boxing gloves, uncoils the fists, lowers the guard, rings the bell, pulls up a comfy chair and offers a glass of iced tea by simply riding their bus.

Barnacles

(You know, those little crustacean thingies that grow on stuff in salt water)

I saw a video of a whale with barnacles all over its head. The whale had just breached right next to a boat full of people, then swam over to the boat and let folks touch it. It was very cool and I hope to have that same experience some day.

When the video was done, my mind wandered to the barnacles the whale had on its head. I saw them, but didn't notice them right away. Meaning, they were clearly in the video, but as I watched it, I didn't realize they were there because quite honestly, it's perfectly normal to see them on whales. As with a lot of things that are regularly seen together, they kind of become one and the same.

The article I read shortly after said that the whale is not hurt or bothered by the barnacles and that it can even use them to do extra damage to rivals in fights. So the whale knows they are there, but puts up with them because they are hard to get rid of and if it gets into a fight, it can use the barnacle covered area as an armored-grater against its foe.

What about us? Our fleshly quirks? Our selfish ability to irritate others?

Are we swimming around with barnacles covering some areas of our lives?

They way I deal with customers, siblings, my annoying neighbors, parents? Am I 'OK' with rough areas because they help defend me? Do I justify being rude because that's just how I am when I'm hungry, tired, lonely? I get it, it is very hard to focus on the rough patches and do the work to get rid of them. It can be scary volunteering to give up our armor.

125

In the Bible, it says that God is our defender and that we should strive to not take offense at the words and actions of others. It goes so far as to say, *"God blesses you when people mock you and persecute you and lie about you and say all sorts of evil things against you because you are my followers. Be happy about it! Be very glad! For a great reward awaits you in heaven. And remember, the ancient prophets were persecuted in the same way."* Matt 5:11-12

BE HAPPY ABOUT IT???   *ARE YOU KIDDING?*

Well, NO. God wants us to trust Him and live like Jesus did. In other words, lose the barnacles.

  I can be prickly about my career, my finances, my relationships, my past and my failures, or I can be obedient to God, live in faith and trust Him to defend me. I can trust Him to point out the barnacles and teach me to break their hold. I can be free!

  I can be free from the barnacle-chains that I have worn for so long. Perhaps, like the whale, I've had them so long that I see myself and them, as <u>one and the same</u>!

'That's just how I am', doesn't need to be my catch-phrase ...ever again.

Seeking fertile ground

There have been many times when I have called out to God, "What am I supposed to do?"

I just wanted to know what God wanted. "C'mon Lord, just tell me please!" Do you know that feeling? After many years of calling out that question with no responses, I began to wonder, is it the wrong question? Maybe our faith walk isn't about getting answers, but about figuring out how to do the right thing, without answers! Oh, I know that's not the way any of us want it to be. Telephone calls from God, with detailed instructions and a timetable! That's what we really want, but where is the actual faith in that? My journey of faith has changed and I now live by some different ideas.

I started using the term '*seeking fertile ground*' several years ago, when I got tired of saying 'I'm trying to figure out what God wants me to do'. It sounded too lost for me I guess. But this new motto has helped me to stay focused since then. After all, isn't that what God wants for me all the time, to be planted where I will grow the best? Not where I will be most comfortable or even happiest, but where I will grow best!!! You will find that I often refer to the fruit of the Spirit in my thought process. I believe it is a much more valuable tool than we usually think.

If I read it right in Galatians 5, God's Spirit grows these things where He is. If God is somewhere and He is having an affect, these 9 things will sprout and be revealed! "*But, the fruit of the spirit is...*" IS!!! Not may be, but most certainly IS! They grow from the presence and power of God and only God. I might be taking a little liberty in my understanding but I think I'm pretty close on this one. The presence, power and moving of God's Spirit WILL result in the appearance and growth of love, joy, peace, patience... in my life. So I want to find the best place to grow them, my fertile ground. One could almost say that in searching out my fertile ground, I may in fact inadvertently also find what God wants me to do.

Perhaps that is the real goal after all. Perhaps all the

'things He wants me to do' have the same purpose, though they differ in details. In everything in this life, might the single common goal be to **help me grow** into being more like Jesus? If yes, then the **fertile ground** is the answer. I must yield myself to God (*as fertile ground for the Holy Spirit*), ready to be planted and look for the situations that match that purpose. *Now, I don't have to go looking in false humility for situations that will hurt me. God isn't asking me to martyr myself.* He's asking me to trust Him in the deepest and hardest sense. In a way that <u>grows the most fruit</u>!

I have to make this point very clear though. Growth means change. Seeking fertile ground will cause you to change. If the goal is to become MORE like Jesus, then I have to change from being so much like ME. No way around it, change and growth, growth and change, stretching our capacities and redefining our faith, our purpose, our habits, our goals and ourselves is probably going to happen. It has to happen!

The head Pastor at the church we attend said once, '*if you don't know what you're supposed to do, go where you see God moving and get involved*'. My wife and I loved that. It went hand-in-hand with 'seeking fertile ground'.

With my new ideas of finding God's plan for me, I have had more adventures, more love, more growth, more fruit and more fun. I used to stand in one place and call out for answers. Now I go with what I know so far and I find what He has for me.

This has not led me to more answers, <u>just fewer questions</u>.

(*Fewer questions sounds nice, doesn't it?*)

I have been amazed how easily He has gotten my attention in this new way of thinking. I guess it's like living warmed up and in the starting blocks, instead of just sitting by the phone and waiting for a call with my slippers on!

Some things

So for a season, my wife and I were in a situation where our work included room and board. I know it sounds great but our version was very restrictive. Even though food was included, it wasn't our choice of food or even how to prepare it. I would not call us 'picky eaters' by any means, but in our previous season, we did have some foods that we regularly ate and some we didn't.

Our host tended to get a bit grumpy with us when she found out that we snuck in food for ourselves and that we spent our own money on it. Okay, she got really angry sometimes. I get it, she knew we didn't get paid very much and didn't really have the money for sneaking in food. She felt like there must have been some other problem in our work relationship for us to be buying food when she had agreed to feed us. What she didn't take into account was that romance requires sacrifice.

"Romance requires sacrifice" - by this I don't mean that my wife makes me give up stuff to prove to her that I love her. Actually, it's ME who demands that I give up stuff for her! My love for her demands that I show her as having greater value to me than anyone else through sacrifices. Going where she wants to eat instead of my choice. Watching the movie she wants to see, instead of my choice. Getting yelled at by an elderly lady for spending money to get a treat that makes my wife smile! I don't believe this view of love is just a 'guy thing'. From my experience, this is how God works with me!

Some things He wants to do for me, ...Himself

There will be lessons and blessings that God works for me, through the body of Christ. There will be some He does through strangers or twists of circumstance. There will be some, where He pulls me aside or sets me apart or even walks me into a desert place, in order to be alone with me. (*Hear that?*) In order <u>to be alone with me</u>!!!

Yes of course these seasons will teach us patience and mature our character. Anyone who travels beside Jesus will be prompted to grow like that. We often make this urging toward growth the main point of our 'set apart' seasons. But hey, let's back up and re-focus on the romance involved!!!

What if we focused on the part where I said, *'in order to be alone with me'*? Oh c'mon, doesn't that make it more intimate and loving, less of a *'do I have to go through this'* kind of thing?

It is those times that should win our hearts. Those times when He hopes we allow Him to prove His love for us through intimate sacrifice. I believe God is more interested in fighting for us, than having us fight for Him.

So what about you? Have you experienced a season of being set aside from the others? A need that the church just hasn't stepped up and dealt with? A prayer for quick deliverance or healing that has been 'unanswered'? Do you have a nagging hole in your heart that needs to be filled?

Some things He just wants to do for you, ...HIMSELF!

Invite him to roll up His sleeves and be your personal provision. You may be surprised how eager He is to do it.

(*See David's view of God in Psalm 103*)

Desperate to compromise

(...In a good way)

I have found that second to my relationship with Jesus, my wife is my biggest relational concern. Meaning, I spend most of my energy working on my relationships in that order: Jesus first, then Millie, then everyone else. I can't lose Jesus. He can't un-choose me. It's not in His nature. My wife can! She can call it quits, walk away and give up. There are plenty of better guys out there, richer, smarter, better looking or more fun, so she could find someone else.

I don't believe we should live in fear of relationships ending. That's not what I'm talking about. It's just an honest assessment that she can leave if she wants to. Knowing this, I put effort into the relationship. OK, I put a lot of effort into it. It has great value to me because I love her, I like her and I am better as us than I am as just me. (*not to mention, in order to honor my 1st love, God, I need to value her and my marriage*)

God is perfect, I don't look for compromise with Him because, well, He is always right! I need to focus on trusting, obeying and submitting to Him. Millie on the other hand is far from perfect (*not as far as me though*) and she has many opinions, preferences and personal issues. She's human! Since we both bring our humanness to the relationship, it is inevitably flawed and leans toward disagreement. A healthy love between us keeps many differences at bay, but sometimes an issue or instance gets a bit prickly between us. Often it's a matter of feeling that something was said wrong or done wrong and our hurts want some kind of justice, a little bit of "I was right and you were wrong". We all have that in us from time to time. Just wanting to say, I was right and you were wrong. It's normal because fair is fair!

Here is the reality, fair is fair! Jesus paid for us to be bought out of slavery to sin and hell. Fair means that we are **His** now. Fair means that since I was completely undeserving, yet completely forgiven, I should extend the same mercy and grace toward others. Fair is fair! Fair also means that since the Creator of the universe honors my right to free will, then I need to honor it in others. Fair is fair. <u>So my wife should be the first and greatest recipient of all this fair that God has extended to me</u>.

When there is a speed bump or glitch in our harmony, my first reaction shouldn't be hoping for "I am right and you are wrong", it should be for a compromise. A healthy, "I will meet you in the middle and we can talk this out, so we both understand each other and can get back to living in the astoundingly generous presence of the God who loves and favors us both", is what we should be aiming for. Both listening. Both understanding. Both valuing the relationship over being right!

Whenever there's uneasiness in the stuff between Millie and I, I go right to compromise. It's my hope that I will always fight for us, over fighting against her.

Stop being Godly

We have to blame my wife for this one. (*You'll see what I mean*)

So here's my problem sometimes. I try so hard to do what's right with God that I sort of forget to be loved. I will clarify for you. There are times when I pray for myself with an "I-don't-deserve-my-salvation-and-forgiveness, so-I-won't-ask-for-anything-else" attitude. Not trying to be self-righteous or beat myself up on purpose, but as my wife pointed out the other day, I pray big and gracious things for others without hesitation because I know God adores them. But, my expectation for myself seems to be that I have acquired my happy ending in heaven by trading it for an UN-happy journey on earth.

What my wife was reminding me of is that I am also on the receiving end of God's adoration. He sent Jesus to buy me back because of His love for ME. Not just because I'm part of the 'all of humanity package' that we read of in John 3:16.

ME.... I am deeply loved by my Father in Heaven. He smiles over me. He sings over me. He stares at me intently every moment of every day. He longs for my company at His house and has great and wondrous plans for me until then. Like any loving father, he appreciates my volunteering to help him, but His love for me is not conditional upon that and it's His great joy to express a love for me that is ridiculously personal and designed to give me a Christmas morning thrill, every day! (*That was harder for me write than you might imagine but it is also, all true*)

My favorite verse is Micah 6:8 do justly, love mercy and walk humbly with your God. My job is not to 'act Godly', but to walk humbly with my God. I need to remember to take off the fake mustache, the official looking tie and throw on the t-shirt that says, "I'm hanging with my DAD".

133

My wife frequently says things that get me to think differently about others, this time it was about myself.

There is not a job that God has for me that is so important that He wants me to lose sight of His even greater love for me. My advice to you: Say the same things to yourself...

(*Go ahead. Read this out loud to yourself*)

ME.... I am deeply loved by my Father in Heaven. He smiles over me. He sings over me. He stares at me intently every moment of every day. He longs for my company at His house and has great and wondrous plans for me until then. Like any loving father, he appreciates my volunteering to help him, but His love for me is not conditional upon that and it's His great joy to express a love for me that is ridiculously personal and designed to give me a Christmas morning thrill, every day! There is not a job that God has for me, that is so important that He wants me to lose sight of His even greater love for me. Amen

The algebra of PLEASE

When I was a school teacher, I taught a lot of different subjects. It was a private school for kids with mild learning disorders, so they needed help getting past a few hurdles understanding certain concepts. I found Algebra to be one of these hard-to-grasp concepts for them. Treating letters as numbers and coming up with answers from equations with variables on both sides of the equal sign. It was like learning a foreign language for them. So we had to deal with that concept barrier before we could learn the skills needed to do algebra.

What I taught them first was how to clean their bedrooms. We discussed what usually happens when a kid is told to clean their room and what tools they might find helpful. I admitted that I always struggled as a kid when cleaning my room because I would find some lost toy or comic book and get distracted. I realized I needed some kind of list of steps to take in order to keep me focused on completing the task at hand. Together, we came up with a new list of steps:
1. Pick up all laundry - put clean clothes in drawers and dirty ones in hamper.
2. Pick up all trash, put in trash can.
3. Pick up all plates and glasses - bring to kitchen sink.

From this point, the lists would vary a bit. They got the idea that the **solution** wasn't finding the solution. The solution was **removing one piece of the problem at a time**. Just as a clean floor is actually already under the disaster of our bedrooms; the answer to an algebraic equation is hidden in the question. It's a logic thing.

I recently had an unusual experience with the algebra of PLEASE. I spent some time living in a place where someone almost always said thank you, but almost never said please. As time passed, I found this imbalance hard to ignore. I knew without a doubt that this person loved Jesus. I also knew that they were in pain almost constantly, so I tried to be patient and understanding, but the way the equation looked to my heart was deeply unbalanced. I found myself critical of their faith. It was a lopsided equation and it hurt my heart. This person would bark out orders and demands at me without saying please. When I completed each task, there would be a gentle 'thank you ' waiting for me. It just didn't sit well with me and I even began questioning the heart of this person because the 'please' and 'thank you' didn't make sense.

My criticalness was a problem between God and me. I didn't voice it to the person. It was my problem, as I said! It was an issue of forgiveness and compassion that God dealt with.

The point here is that this persons inconsistency looked like a broken faith to me. I found myself asking God to reveal to me where my own faith is unbalanced. I don't want to live a life that is a broken algebraic equation. People should look at my life and be able to make sense of it. They should be able to say, "He says he believes in Jesus and wants to follow Him and that is exactly what I see".

If our life and faith are an unbalanced equation, people may think that our faith is bad math! We should be able to follow the 'math-example' that Jesus lived out everyday.

My list for this has 3 rules that are found in Micah 6:8:
1. Do justly - always treat others with the honor and respect that they deserve as children of God.
2. Love mercy - prefer forgiveness and kindness in every unfair situation.
3. Walk humbly with your God - take His hand like a little kid and spend each day going where He leads.

Unnamed supporting cast

So here's a question that I believe God is asking all of us.

Would you give up being the main character in your own story to be a 'walk on character' in someone else's story?

If God asked you to, would you do it?

(*I'm not talking about being a parent, because your child is part of your story*)

A stranger. Just a somebody-else's-story kind of thing.

Could we let God close our book for right now and let Him write us into someone else's story as a character without a name? With just a he or she for a title. Just for a few pages or a short chapter?? My wife and I recently had a chapter like that where God plopped us down in someone else's story as a caregiver for an elderly lady. We cleaned, made meals according to specific directions, drove errands at a moments notice, slept with a baby-monitor on every night and spent all our other time sitting and waiting to be called on for anything else. Can God count on us to volunteer as an 'Unnamed supporting cast member' in any story He wants??? I want Him to be able to count on me like that, but gee-whizz that's a lot to ask.

Jesus volunteered! In every person's life that doesn't acknowledge Him as Lord, He is simply a '*he*'.

He never complains about being ignored or *unnamed*. If we want to be more like Jesus, I think we have to accept more unnamed roles in the lives of others.
(*...once again...*)

"If we want to be more like Jesus, I think we have to accept more unnamed roles in the lives of others!"

- John 3:30 *"He must become greater; I must become less."*

...How about an unnamed supporting cast member, in your own story? Maybe that's the end goal for all of us while we're on earth. Taking a backseat in our own lives? Jesus did that. WOW, that's a pretty high standard to shoot for. How are we supposed to give up our fun, our dreams, our prosperity, our friends, our career, our fortunes and our desires everyday, just to make God happy? *It does sound like that's what He's asking us to do.* Unless you see this one factor a little bit differently.

Perhaps God is saying, ***"I will hold your fun, your dreams, your prosperity, your friends, your career, your fortunes and your desires for you. I will take them from this place of sin and decay and I will place them where there is no sin and no decay. Because I love you and you are trusting me with these things of yours, I will multiply them for you a thousand times and make them so they never fade away."*** *The conviction of typing that made me tear-up).*

It's called Heaven! We don't seem to get the idea that heaven is more than just the PLACE of rest and reward. It's also the TIME of rest and reward. If we're on this earth breathing, there is still work to do. God doesn't tell us we have to give up our today's, but He does invite us to trade them for the promised tomorrows. Is that fair? Heck no!!!! We make out like bandits in the deal! Getting something of a much greater value, greater quality and quantity than we could ever acquire on our own! Trade up today's pleasures for those of eternity and trade up your life, for His.

A puzzle piece in the wrong box

Can you imagine putting a jigsaw puzzle together, only to find a piece in the box that belonged with a different puzzle? Frustrating for sure, but I have to tell you, I believe that I am that piece that doesn't belong, and it's fine with me. Well, it is now. It hasn't been a pretty journey, but I get why God brought me here the long way.

I grew up believing, like many people do, that family should be close and nobody can take their place. It is part of the American culture to think 'blood is thicker than water'. (*A term meaning that nobody could ever love you or be as close to you, as biological family can*) We heard it in movies and TV shows and books. Family struggled but eventually always remembered to love each other most. It's a closeness that survives every tragedy and every distance, that is what we would always hope for and reach for. Finally, we would always return HOME, just as birds and turtles do, instinctively, because that is how it's supposed to be. Right?

I found this an impossible goal that left me hurt and full of self-doubt. What was the real problem with me connecting with my family? Lots of folks get past feeling awkward and misunderstood as a child, to eventually find their place in the family puzzle. I guess I'm not one of those people. The more I try to connect, the more I feel like I am a puzzle piece in the wrong box.

I have to say, this is not the fault of my family. They always leave a spot for me, but I just don't seem to fit. It's like I was born with a different heart-language in me, or something. They aren't wrong, I'm just not right for their puzzle. For a long time, I wanted to fit in so bad. I would try to connect on levels that I thought would be a sure place of mutual interest or experience, but it always felt like an uneasy acquaintance and not what I thought family should feel like.

I believe that in some cases, 'family' is not so much about your last name or where you were born. It's about who helps you to 'be alive'. My wife said once, "*I don't understand my family, I'm just related to them!*"

(Follow me out into the garden for a minute)

Many seedlings are transplanted far from where they started. Read that one again, nice and slow. MANY SEEDLINGS ARE TRANSPLANTED FAR FROM WHERE THEY STARTED. *(The gardener/Jesus knows where we are most needed and where we will grow best)* That's me, a transplanted seedling and it might be you too. If so, please don't let it hurt too much. There are reasons why God transplants some people, though it usually requires us stepping back to get a bigger picture of the entire garden to understand why.

Why do I think God allowed me to "not fit in"? I'd love to share my guess with you.

If my life had the emotional security of fitting in, of feeling accepted and understood. I wouldn't understand the feelings of those Jesus came to reach. The broken hearted and hopeless. The misfits and outcasts! I would not understand their shame and pain, which might make my faith too shallow for them to connect to. Instead, I walk in their shoes. I cry their tears and I know the God they need! **Hallelujah for my brokenness, it is my honor to represent the broken to God in my prayers and to represent God to them, in my tears!** Taking the long way here with Jesus has made me a better me.

The last point to make is an easy one. Jesus, living in paradise, in perfect harmony with the Father and the Spirit, left home. He left union of the most perfect kind. He chose instead to be misunderstood, lonely, a misfit and a puzzle piece from the wrong box! Jesus knew it was the only way to show the empathy and compassion of God toward His wayward children.

He understands us and wants me to understand 'us' too.

The last Salvation!

This idea came up one day when I was kicking around some thoughts on the 'End Times'. I'm not one of those Christians who spends very much time trying to figure out all the hidden mysteries of the second coming of Jesus. What I like to do is kick around some weird *"if that's true, **then** it must also mean"* situations based on Bible facts.

So, *The LAST Salvation* is one of those hypothetical things. (*It is not doctrine. It is not truth. It is only an idea, so please take it as that*). I don't remember what spurred the thought. I just know that at one point I was thinking, "**what could be keeping Jesus from coming back?**" (*Good question right?*) My understanding of the end times events are based on what I was taught, and not what I know. I know there are different views of the timetable and the meanings of things mentioned in the Bible. So please forgive any errors I make against your understanding and just accompany me to the end of this idea.

So, that seed thought, "What could be keeping Jesus from coming back?" Then this thought popped into my head. **"He is waiting until everyone has a chance to get saved."** (*Based on 2 Peter 3:9-10, Romans 1:18-20*) In these verses, we get the theological idea that God says ALL people either HAVE or WILL HAVE the chance to know Him and get saved before He has Jesus come back to get us and deal with all the wrongs on this sad, broken planet. NOBODY will have an excuse. *Lord, I am looking forward to your return.*

Why is it taking so long? "God, I know you see all the suffering, the pain and the evil. I know that nothing escapes your sight and that you feel our hurts. You see the injustice. Why, oh why, do you wait?" (*I am sure most of us have days or seasons of asking these very same questions*) Then I think of MY Jesus (*you will hear me refer to Him that way frequently*) and how He has revealed his nature and character to me through His Word, His creation and His walk

with me. He is kind, patient and faithful!!! So why is he
waiting to return?

Can we picture it like this?
Is He waiting for the last salvation???

If Jesus is waiting to come back.
If He is waiting for everyone to have a chance to get saved.
If He is heartbroken over all who will be lost.
If He is patient and kind.
...then we can guess that He wants this all to be over too.

He wants to make things right and wipe away all tears.

Since people get saved by their individual decision, it's fair to
guess that there will be a last person to make that decision.
A last salvation! A very last person letting Jesus in!
Somewhere there will be a final witness, a final word of
encouragement, a final person asking another person,
"Would you like to accept Jesus as your personal Lord and
Savior?"
So, is that my job or is it written for **you** to do? Maybe
the kid in our Sunday school class will have that honor?

Oh my. If this guess is true, then how will we conduct our
lives from this point forward?

Are we actively working toward the last salvation?
I hope we both are!

Frozen Jesus dinner

Please understand that I write this as a question for myself, the way I share my Jesus. I know that it may sound as if I am being harsh on my church or the global Body of Christ. I am not. I see the Holy Spirit moving and the church I attend is kind and miraculous.

My concern is more for the wisdom I may be missing.

I spend a lot of time thinking about what's missing in our approach to kids ministry. Why is it that so few kids catch the spark and run with God, instead of stumbling into adolescence and face planting into adulthood? Is it inevitable that 85% of kids who get saved or attend Sunday school, find their faith hollow and powerless just a few years later?

If that's true, then nearly everyone is doomed to the hard path. Doomed to making the worst decisions, feeling the deepest pains and causing the most hurts to others. C'mon, that can't be true can it? Please Lord show us how to reach kids better.

In Gen 22, we read about Abraham going up the mountain to sacrifice Isaac. Most scholars figure Isaac was around 12-19 years old at that time. Which would make him the most compliant and unusual teenager <u>ever</u>!!! Perhaps though, he was just a teenager of **unusual faith**. He had heard his father's story repeatedly and more important than that, he had seen his father and mother's faith in action, both the victories and the failures. God must have been real to Isaac because of the life he lived with his family and the journey they shared together. No teen ever showed that type of respect or obedience because of an "*I said so, that's why!*" type of family dynamic. Is that what we're missing: a real faith relationship on display, a faith for the whole family to participate in?

When I first started walking with God, I was attending a church of "we're right and everyone else is wrong, so we do it the way we've always done it." (*I saw it fail so many kids and families*) I now see churches make a more inclusive church-culture, using words like "community, tribe and un-churched". (*I have seen that fail too*) Of course my own story as a father is a story of great failure as well. I tried so hard to make my own kids live the right kind of life that I drove them away from faith. It was not my best chapter. They made the decision to attribute my failings to the God I claimed to serve. I understand why they did that, even though it isn't fair to God.

WHAT WAS I MISSING? What went wrong?

My second wife and I spent 4 months working at a maternity house for teenagers. 120 hours in a row, per week, with 4 pregnant teens! It was wonderfully brutal. These were girls that didn't want the faith we had to offer them. They only wanted whatever free stuff the program gave them and not any of our Jesus-y advice.

So how do we make faith intimate and practical and real and magical, all at the same time, for each kid, each teen?

(Follow my side thoughts for a second please)

Frozen TV dinners have changed so much over the years. The first ones I remember were all wrapped in aluminum foil, tasted like some kind of gravy-ish mush and always burned your mouth. They were the 'solution' for busier families. Now, TV dinners come in recycled containers, look like actual food, have less sodium, are prepared in smaller batches and are made with REAL ingredients. Still a 'solution' for 'busy' families.

They are also not the right solution. Merely '**a better wrong solution**'. I wonder sometimes if our packaged church cultures are just a better wrong solution. We buy curriculums that are mass-produced. Songs that fit the pop-culture tempo and 'farm-out' summer camps to those who are better equipped to be Jesus-y to the collection of kids coming to our church. OH, and they say the number of kids increases when we offer better prizes.

Just heat up one of those Frozen Jesus Dinners!

YES, I know, it sounds harsh and I am sorry for that. I know that kids are different these days. I know they are more into electronics and less into real conversation. I am just concerned that a newer or better solution for reaching our kids for Jesus may not be the **right** solution. Please understand that I am not saying that I have the answer, just that I have seen crowds accidentally choose their popular ideas, over God. I've even seen a Godly crowd do it. I think the key is making sure you are giving them your Jesus, not a prepackaged one. Kids can tell if you really know and believe in the Jesus that you're trying to sell them, or if you're just giving them some up-to-date church experience.

That being said, my heart always leaps back to Jesus saying, "*if I be lifted up, I will draw all men unto me*" (*Jn 12:32*). I mean, Paul knew the word of God and the religious songs and he had no idea who God really was or how to live the life God had for him, until his 'church culture' got the crap kicked out of it!   Scrapped like a bad plan.

(*3 years in the wilderness with Jesus to unlearn religion*)

The Apostle Paul needed a crash course in the return to what the faith really meant. It was never supposed to be about the 'popular church culture' of any age, but a gathering of folks focused on the 'God & me' thing. Unity in our faith isn't supposed to be us agreeing with each other on the 5 steps of church building and multimedia methods. God gave us our unity in Christ, OUR UNITY IS IN CHRIST. We just need to "endeavor to keep it". (*Eph 4:3-5*)

145

I would say it's all about KEEPING OUR UNITY and DISCOVERING YOUR INDIVIDUALITY.

By Paul's time, the faith of Israel had become a strong religion full of tradition and culture. They had forgotten that it began with Abram stumbling around, chasing a single voice that offered to touch and bless his soul. That is what Paul needed, to meet a God who could set him free from his religion. Jesus was 'lifted up' (*on a cross*) above Paul's religion and FAITH finally became real!

May we all continue to seek God for the right way to live our faith in front of others so they can also grow to have what Isaac had, <u>an unusual faith and not a frozen Jesus dinner</u>.

The splash zone

There's this great big 'splash-zone' in the Bible story of Luke 11:17-19.

Ten lepers were healed and only one of them came back and thanked Jesus. The other nine were allowed to keep their healings without expressing any gratitude at all. These 'free-loaders' walked away from the King of Kings thinking only about them selves. What they had just gotten was an undeserved miracle that may have just fallen on them because one worthy soul cried out and they happened to be standing next to him when God opened the window of healing from heaven. Do I know that to be true?

Nope, but I don't know it's not true either.

Ok so the story is that Jesus and His disciples were walking on toward the next town, Jerusalem. As they got to the part of the road where the border between Galilee and Samaria was, ten lepers appeared but kept a safe distance. They began to yell for Jesus. "Jesus, Master, have mercy on us!" He looked at them and said, "Go show your selves to the priests" and as they walked away they were all healed.

One of the healed people was overcome when he noticed his disease was gone and turned around, coming back to Jesus. He yelled, "Praise God!" and fell at the feet of Jesus thanking Him. This man was a Samaritan, an interracial people that the Jews were supposed to ignore, even hate, yet he was the only one to say *"thank you"*.

Personal question for you and be honest - Have you ever been in a situation where God has blessed more than you would've liked. Yes, I know how that sounds, it sounds selfish and mean. But I can admit that there have been times when I was upset with God's generosity and found it to be wildly unfair.

I'm talking about doing your best, while others are doing the least they can get away with and then someone gives a reward to everyone. Do you know what I mean? One of those unfair times where the majority gets some blessing that is really only deserved by an individual. There, I said it!

We all know that it's true and we've all felt that way and inside we yelled, "it's not fair God!" We want a comparison scale, a way to rank us from best to worst so God doesn't mess up when He hands out blessings and His favor! The splash zone isn't how we picture an orderly or fair God operating.

But, Jesus is always pushing us to repaint our picture of God and in that, allow God to redefine us too. We are after all, created in His image.

Let's re-examine one paragraph from earlier...

These 'free-loaders' walked away from the King of Kings, thinking only about them selves. What they had just gotten was an undeserved miracle that may have just fallen on them because one worthy soul cried out and they happened to be standing next to him when God opened the window of healing from heaven.

Couldn't that be said of our own salvations? How about our entire lives? When have we ever been deserving or sufficiently thankful? I admit that I am a freeloader of mercy and grace. I was close to the heart of Jesus when his death opened the window of heaven and reigned down mercy like a flood. We are all just recipients of God's splash zone and nothing else!

Gypsy lifestyle

(A calling lost?)

My wife and I have had a journey that some friends refer to as a *'gypsy lifestyle'*. Never knowing what God wants from us on most things and often leaping toward what we call nudges or leadings, without having all our ducks in a row. That's the part that we're talking about right now, the unanswered, undefined, unclear, unsure things that we seem to volunteer for.

When I was in Bible College, we all threw the word "called" around a lot. "God's **called** me to be a Youth Pastor." "God's **called** me to be a missionary." "God's **called** me to be or do or whatever!" As I look back to that time, I really thought that God had called me to be a youth pastor. I thought His plan for me was to have that job, that title and that position. That was when I was in my 20's. I'm in my 50's now!!! Did I do something wrong? Have I missed my chance? Did He find someone else to take my place??? All good questions but probably missing the point entirely.

I think the real point is that God **has called me**. Just not to a title or position. He has called me <u>His beloved</u>. He has called me <u>son</u>. He has called me <u>forgiven and free</u>.
His beloved son, forgiven and free!

Could there be a higher calling, a greater purpose a clearer direction? Nope. Ok, so that calms down my quest to find my unique purpose. It establishes that I am already unique in Him. From there I look for how He wants me to be. How He wants me to be? Could that be my big 'do'? ***Is the thing God designed me to do, as simple as figuring out <u>how He wants me to be</u>?***

I believe that **is** the secret right there. Be how He wants you to be and you will find all the DOs lining up in front of you. This brings us to my 'life-verse', Micah 6:8,

"...Do justly, love mercy and walk humbly with your God". It actually says in the Bible that this is what the Lord requires of you (*of us*). Perhaps they are the prerequisites for standing right in the center of the spotlight that illuminates our paths. You know when you hear something from just one side of you and you turn to face the sound to hear it better, to find the source? Maybe doing justly, loving mercy and walking humbly with our God is exactly what puts us dead-center in the middle of the great stereo, surround-sound, Dolby presence of the Holy Spirit!

Ok, now I have to take all this back to the gypsy thing right?

I used to think I was called to a position, but I never got that title. Thankfully, I have been blessed to be used for 30 years to do the teaching, leading and loving of a lot of kids.
(*So I ask myself, which has more honor, **the title** or **the work**?*)

I no longer have any idea at all what I'm called to do. I only know how I'm called to be. That is my focus and I have more peace. This revelation brings me to a steady heart in an unsteady life. I find myself responding more quickly to things that I believe the Spirit of God nudges me about. (*change that person's flat tire, buy that guy lunch, help that lady with her groceries, go visit them, lend a hand there, give a kind word here, tell them that Jesus loves them*) This new view tends to keep me from having a '*that's not my job, I'm called to something else*' attitude. It leaves me more open to God and me doing things that I never planned on doing. I don't jump to questions like, "do I have the money in savings to cover that? Should I stay where it's safe and not risk change? Will I have enough for me? Shouldn't I buy a house? Do I have enough to retire? <u>Is there a net to catch me</u>?"

Instead I find just 3 questions rolling around my head, am I doing justly, am I loving mercy and am I walking humbly with my God? These questions leave me (*us*) vulnerable to a wild and passionate breeze when God's Spirit blows whithersoever He wants. Are we ready to walk away from wherever here is, into the unknown? A gypsy lifestyle!

Now, the other side of the coin:

Do I like this gypsy lifestyle? No! At times, it's hard and hurts and gives me little voices that call me irresponsible and a poor provider. I adore my Sweety and want to give her everything she deserves, a home to call her own, financial security, health insurance, vacations, a car that's less than 20 years old... (*you get it*). It can also terrify me on the inside, the lack of control, the lack of confidence in myself and my plans. The kingdom of Russ is a shabby little tent.

Don't get me wrong there are serious positives too. We have had some unbelievable adventures doing things that we had no right to be a part of, the intense love of some of the greatest people we've ever known, lot's of experience leaning on the promises and character of God and we have become the best Russ and Millie that either of us has ever been! So again I ask myself, do you like this gypsy lifestyle? NO, but I love the way it refines me and makes me grow into a better reflection of my Jesus! There, I guess my calling is finally found, be like Jesus.

Here's the simple math of it all.

God has promised the next life is full of Joy, Love and Security FOREVER!

No tears, no pain and no FAITH.

This life here on earth is my one chance to abandon myself and earthly wisdom, and to walk with my Savior completely based on faith. There is no faith in Heaven because sin (*and flesh*) will be gone and we will all be perfect once we get there. We will also see God, face to face.

The idea of trying to get my security here and now, knowing this world and it's riches will all be gone one day, goes against faith doesn't it? God invites us to be like Abraham and follow Him to a place we have never been before. He invites us to do the foolish, doesn't make sense, we have no proof, just hope and faith thing. <u>That is the invitation</u>! What will we say to God? *"Uhhm, thanks but I'd rather collect things that I'm going to lose in the years to come"* or *"I'm really scared of what could happen Lord, but if you already have my destiny secured, then ok, let's do this!"*

Remember, there is no faith in heaven. There's no need for it! Our only chance to live by faith, the only thing that pleases God in Hebrews 11:6, is while we're here on earth.

RIGHT NOW, FAITH and the gypsy lifestyle.

Train or the tunnel?

I was fortunate enough once, to visit a gentleman with an impressive train room. He had a huge village set up with mountains and tunnels and working lights. it was the whole deal. (*I do like trains*) As I watched the trains going around, I thought, how fun it would be to bring my little action camera and strap it to the top of the train. I mean, watching the train go through a tunnel is cool, but to see it from the train's point of view would be cooler right? I thought so.

As often happens in my brain, things sort of popped into place for this next thought. We have **life** and we have **faith**. One is supposed to enhance the other. One is supposed to be more important than the other. According to the lessons of Jesus... (*I think*) one is the train and one is the tunnel! YES, that happens in my brain quite often.

Does my faith run through my life or does my life run through my faith?

If my life is my big thing and my faith is just something I pass through it, then my faith is an adjective to my life? "*My name is Russ, I was born in New York State, I am short, I like to draw, I am remarried, I like the beach and kayaking and I am a Christian.*" Do I only use my faith when it suits me, when it's convenient, when it's advantageous, when it's <u>not</u> <u>embarrassing</u>? Do I carve a path through my life, to allow faith a safe passage only where I want it to go? God forbid - (*I hope this makes sense to you*)

On the other hand, if my faith is the big thing, then my life is allowed to pass through it, directed by it, protected by it, <u>submitted to the path it dictates</u>. Oh, if only my faith were the mountain, this huge immoveable mountain. A force bigger than my train, defining my path! I would have the kind of life that Jesus invited us all to have. A huge abundant life that honestly works beyond rules and reason. Some would look and shake their heads at how absurd it is, putting my faith as my mountain over my life. Onlookers would want to know 'how it works', this faith that **costs me everything-mine** and **gives me everything-HIS**!

I want my life, my existence, my hours, dreams and choices to be run through my faith for approval and guidance. Allowing my life to fit into my faith, <u>instead of my faith fitting into my life</u>. I think Jesus made it clear which was His tunnel and which His train.

Can I ask you to prayerfully consider which is bigger, your faith or your life?

Leave it there

I am not going to assume that my Grandma is in heaven just because I hope she's there and I really did love her a lot. (*That's kinda cold Russ. What's with the attitude?*) I know it's a hard topic to be honest about, but we have to, we just have to. God is Holy and Righteous and not a respecter of persons and a million other verses about His ways being higher than mine and those who cry 'Lord, Lord' and He says 'I never knew you'. (*sigh*) I want my Grandma to be in heaven but I'm not sure if she is. I didn't know her well enough to have seen the fruit of a relationship with Jesus, in her story. But, I HOPE she's in heaven!

Salvation is a huge thing to leave to hope when it's someone you love, but it isn't my decision and my prayers can't push someone through the gates, it doesn't work that way. So, whose decision is it? Well, it's not mine and really, it's not God's. I AM TOTALLY SERIOUS, IT'S NOT GOD'S DECISION. HE DOESN'T CHOOSE WHO MAKES IT INTO HEAVEN AND WHO DOESN'T! God already made His choice and He said, "Yes, I want them all to come home". That's His decision and His deep and passionate desire. Here's the catch, we have to choose it too. Everyone has to make their own choice and the 'deal' has certain terms, but God already signed the paperwork on the cross. The pen is now in our hands.

My Grandma had to choose for herself and my love for her didn't (*and doesn't*) mean anything to the deal. It doesn't affect her chance at salvation at all. (*dang Russ, just getting all hardball on us with this tough subject*) No, actually this is all leading up to a great revelation. My love doesn't matter in this, but the entire deal was bought by the love of God!!! God's love is bigger, brighter, warmer, stronger, deeper, wider, longer, higher, more pure and a billion times more personal and intimate toward my grandma than mine was. Oh thank you God, thank you! The rest was in her court. He did it all, He gave the offer and chased her every day of her life and declared His love for her. I can, and have to, <u>leave it there</u>.

We all have to leave it there. Nobody's Nana is now an Angel. 'Good people' don't automatically make it to heaven. Yes, there is a hell and it isn't empty. There are facts and rules about heaven, no matter what we would like it to be like, no matter what our religion of choice might give us for options and no matter how we think some people compare with others. I guess all of that would be bad news and a hopeless situation, except for the other fact. That God's love is bigger, brighter, warmer, stronger, deeper, wider, longer, higher, more pure and a billion times more personal and intimate toward those we love, than ours ever could be.

So, here's the Bible story that I keep tucked in my shirt close to my heart. Luke 23:33-43, the thief on the cross NEXT to Jesus. Is that not a picture of how far and how hard Jesus chases each of us? Right up to the point of death. If that is the Jesus who loved my Grandma, then I can leave HER story, in HIS hands and know that He is good and kind and just. I can't say that I know she's in heaven because I don't know her choice, I only know God's love.
But, **I can leave it there, because I trust Him**.

I hope my Grandma is in heaven. I hope she saw the love that chased her every day and said yes to it. I hope she had the joy of walking with Jesus until she awoke in His arms and I will just leave it all right there, in the hands of the most amazing, generous and loving person I have ever met.
My Jesus!

Declassified files

(Declassified means: officially declare information or documents to no longer be secret)

Declassified files would suggest that there is and was special information that has been kept secret or withheld from common knowledge. Stories that were hidden from plain view and things that happened without most people ever knowing about them, <u>probably even being officially denied until the moment they become declassified</u>!

We often see this term used for reports on military actions that were taken in secret. Sometimes, a movie will be made about an amazingly brave team of heroes who were never given credit for doing something that secretly saved a lot of lives. The question could be asked, why were their actions a secret in the first place? As we find out when all the details come to light, often the actions taken were without following all of the rules of the local governments. Sometimes actions were done in secret to protect innocent people or they didn't want their plans to be leaked out to the bad guys. There's always a reason for keeping it secret! Sometimes it's a good reason, sometimes it's not, because we are all human and can make mistakes.

<u>God, however, does not make mistakes</u>. A day is coming when all that has been done in secret will be explained. It will all make perfect sense and there will be a big, "*Oooooh, now I get it*", from all of us. There are several types of things that fall into God's classified information. The time of the Rapture, the day we are each going to die, exactly what heaven will look like and who will be there. For me, these are classified files that I am not concerned with because I know He is just and kind and will keep all of His promises. There are other classified files that I am looking forward to hearing about, those concerning regular people who walk with God. I want to know their secret-hero stories!

Maybe the declassified files will go something like this...

There's a lady who has been in a wheelchair for the last 32 years. She's stuck at home and has very little money.

It seems like she is limited in her usefulness to those around her and to God. We find out that when she was 27, she gave her life to Jesus and told Him that she was willing to do whatever He wanted. 2 years later she got a disease that left her unable to walk. It seemed the devil had struck a blow against her, but what we didn't know was that God had planned to use this physical limitation to train her as a prayer warrior! She became so powerful in prayer that she prayed 312 people into situations where they got saved, she prayed 17 people into a place of miraculous healing, she prayed an entire church into a place of greater sacrifice and service to those in need and her example of great joy in infirmity, inspired 37 others with physical limitations, to be prayer warriors too. Her recognition as an amazing faith-hero won't come until her story is declassified in heaven. How about...

A man who decided to walk with God, even though his wife and kids said no.

A woman who can't have kids but gives her life to serve them.

An older gentleman who volunteers every chance he gets.

A child with disabilities, who always chooses to be kind, even to bullies.

A couple that visits their neighbors every week to make sure they're alright.

An abused spouse who tries to make life safe for the kids.

A girl who gives birth to a child that everyone told her to abort.

...all of them declassified one day to reveal the secret heroes they truly are!

Just as your story will one day be declassified, so don't give up, God is for you and He knows what's really going on.

The math of your path

Some folks have called God, 'The Great Mathematician' because there is so much order, science and wisdom to all of His designs. From the design of cells to the movement of the universe, it all declares the math and wisdom of our all-powerful Creator.

The word trajectory means: *the path followed by a projectile flying or an object moving under the action of given forces.*
In other words, when something is thrown, the path it will take is affected by the force of the throw, the pull of gravity and the resistance of the wind. They are all factors that can change the (*path*) **trajectory.** These will then change where it lands. The trajectory will determine if we hit our target!!! If we want to hit our 'targets' in life, we have to plan our trajectories with skill.
Does that make sense?   Good.

God gives us a lot of wisdom-tools in the Bible. We are supposed to grab them and use them to figure out our best, safest-path, **our trajectory**. Actually FIRST, <u>we are supposed to use God's wisdom to pick our targets in life</u>. We should be listening to the wisdom of God concerning all our targets. Our relationship targets, health targets, spiritual targets, social targets, financial targets, everything. God tells us what targets are best from the choices all around us. If we can take God's wise advice on our targets, goals and dreams, then we can seek Him for the wisdom for our trajectory, to reach those targets! (*in cartoon form, that is a kid at a carnival with his Dad, looking around for the best prize in the ring-toss game and then concentrating as he aims and throws his ring for that very prize*)
That was the plan from the beginning, God mentoring mankind to reach our very best! He wanted to shepherd us through the difficulties and dangers of this world.
We said, "No!"

Now I have to tell you, from God's point of view, I'm sure it's all pretty cut and dry. He told us what was good and how to get it. Simple! We just seem to make this simple stuff all complicated. That's what sin does. It messes up our spiritual alignment and we roll toward trouble. (*quite naturally and for the rest of our lives*)

Since we know that we roll toward trouble and our flesh is prone to leaving the wisdom of God, you would think we would arrange our lives around staying focused on His wisdom. We should clear out a bunch of distractions and make sure that all the things in our lives work toward the targets that we are trying to reach. That sounds easy right? Move the things out of the way that are blocking your path to the target (*your trajectory*).

See, God didn't want it to be hard for us. He wanted it to be easy. In the Garden of Eden, He would walk around with Adam during the cool of the day and talk about what is good and how things really are (*from His point of view*), how they really, really are. It was supposed to be our Heavenly Dad and us, at the ring-toss, aiming for the best prize!!!

Satan got involved because he hates us and he hates the love God has for us. He tricked Adam and Eve into trying to figure things out on their own. God gives us a book of wisdom and instructions <u>guaranteed to work</u> and, we throw it aside. It's no wonder that we often miss our targets. Are there things, or even people, that are blocking the path (*trajectory*) to your Godly target?

Treating the symptoms

(We must start with this thought)

"There is great wisdom in serving and praising and growing together. The UNITY God gives us is to help us be and do more together, than we could do separately!"
Eph 4:3, Jn 17:11, 1Pet 3:8, Col 2:19 - UNITY is from God.
We *don't make Unity. We only endeavor to* <u>keep it</u>.

I worked in the O.R. at a hospital for several years. A lot of the people I worked with were wonderful, caring people. I found out though, that the healthcare industry is sometimes just about the money. Instead of trying to cure illnesses, some companies (*only some*), work to find ways to treat the symptoms, to make people feel better, without actually stopping the illness. That allows them to continue to treat you and charge you for a longer period of time.
(Forgive me for what sounds like a moral judgment. That's not what this is about)
I want to swing this over to a spiritual application and I'm not going to be talking about the sin-nature issue in all of us. The Bible made it very clear that even though Jesus completely dealt with the future judgment aspect of our sin-nature, the poison aspect that creeps out of us at every chance will not be dealt with until we leave our earthly bodies for heaven. I'm talking more about how Christians often deal with the disease of a <u>'lack of Christ-likeness'</u> by reading more books, going to more conferences and adopting more popular churchy programs. (*Often attempts to boost unity, inspire greater effort and increase attendance*)

I have to clarify that I have nothing against books, conferences, attendance or programs and they are not automatically wrong
I am just going to be honest about the fact that it's possible for churches and Christians to miss the mark, to get

it wrong, even while reading the Bible, singing Praise and doing VBS (Vacation Bible School).

Jesus did a lot more helping and serving, and a lot less quoting scripture and wearing matching T-shirts, than we often do!!! Scripture is meant to be LIVED, not thrown at people! *Let me just repeat that simple point...*

"Jesus did a lot more helping and serving and a lot less quoting scripture and wearing matching T-shirts than we often do!!! Scripture is meant to be LIVED, not thrown at people!" (*For the record, I am telling myself this one too*)

We need a 'relationship' with Jesus! Now let's park it there for a quick second. *"It's a relationship, not a religion"*, has been a churchy-catch-phrase for a while now and honestly, I am sort of against *churchy-catch-phrases*: "*the un-churched, it's a relationship not a religion, name it and claim it ...etc.*" I feel like they are an exclusive lingo and make the church more of an organized club and less of the thrilling beautiful mess that the New Testament church was; breathing, moving, reaching, sacrificing, struggling and thriving. Chasing the Holy Spirit at full speed, willing to jump and trip and crawl if needed! That being said, I absolutely agree that it's all about having a relationship with Jesus and not being a religious Christian. Just because someone is related to you doesn't mean you have a good relationship with them. We probably all have proof of that in our own families. So, we need to stop pretending that just because we belong to God, we automatically live in close relationship with Him!

When we see a lack of Christ-likeness in ourselves, a lack of the fruit of the Spirit (*Gal 5:22-23*) or any other symptom of a struggling relationship, we need to go to HIM, not a program. Go to God. Fix your relationship with Him! (*a simple truth that we overlook. Why? Because books and conferences and programs are easier than surrender, listening and changing!*)

John 10:10 *paraphrased* (*Jesus had a mission when he came to earth. It was to help us live... NO, REALLY LIVE, BIGGER-EPIC-WORLD CHANGING, LIKE HE DID!*)

Hebrews 4:16 *paraphrased* (*We have full access to the Throne of God, because of Jesus! BOLDLY GO THERE AND ASK!!!*)

Philippians 4:9 *paraphrased* (*Keep doing all the things you see people, who are close to God, doing! DON'T WAIT JUST GO DO THEM!!!*)

Consider these 3 thoughts together. God wants to help us live BIGGER, like Him, connected to Him freely because of His paying for our, now instant, access to His heavenly power so that we can do NOW, what He showed us and asked us to do.

(Sort of the cure for the world's problems right?)

I notice God's word doesn't say train for 8 years, read these 12 books and then you can get a little bit of heaven's power to practice doing some good. He says, <u>do what I did</u>!!!

Oh and also for the record, I DO wear church team T-shirts and go to church conferences. I just don't expect them to be the pinnacle of how I relate to Jesus or communicate Him to the world and <u>I don't expect God's plan for my church experience and me, to be a copy of anyone else's</u>.

I have my own DNA, from God, so why would I expect my 'God experience' to be less unique? (*another disclaimer: I am saying some dangerous stuff here that can be misused, so be very careful how independent you decide to live - God gives us unity through His son and He tells us to carefully KEEP it*) There is great wisdom in serving and praising and growing together and the unity God gives us is to help us be and do more together than we could do separately!!!!!

HE made us a <u>family</u> called the church, not a business. I'm not saying don't do VBS or conferences. (*I personally do every VBS I can*) Do them out of love alone and not counting on them to be the change you and your church need.

Don't put churchy things in the place of Jesus!

Extra prayers needed

I apologize if I offend anyone with this view on prayer. In my journey, I have been exposed to many differing points of view on the subject and my particular broken places have nudged me into this. I have found a lot of peace in my current view, while also setting the bar higher for my faith. Since I first became God's, my understandings of prayer, it's purposes, power and subtleties has changed greatly and I am sure they will continue to change.

My observations fall into 2 categories for this one. 'What people say and do' and 'what God says we should say and do'. Sadly, in the area of prayer, these 2 categories don't seem to line up at times. That being said, it is because of human nature, sin, culture, family example and our earthly realities, that we fall for the lie that *'do more, get more'*, is how prayer works. But, that isn't part of God's economy.

By God's economy, I mean the way He works stuff, His operating system, His mission statement, His company goals and the way He plans on reaching those goals, how He does business, His currency and the things He places value on.

Observation 1 -

'Do more, get more' - it's how we handle school, jobs, relationships, hobbies, fortune and fame. Almost everything in our lives falls into 'do more to get more'. If I put more effort into something, my results will be bigger or better. (*it's almost a law of nature*) If ants work harder, their nest and colony will be larger and stronger. If I work more hours at my job, I will make more money. If I study harder at school, I will get better grades. I won't deny that it applies in many areas.

But, that doesn't mean that God is limited to our understanding or our rules. The laws of nature bow to Him! Not the other way around.

Observation 2 -

Think of Jesus and what he did. He volunteered to leave heaven, be born a baby, live a man's life and die on the cross for a lot of people who hated Him. He bought our freedom from the power and eternal consequences of sin. He bought our invitation to heaven forever. He bought our right to live without guilt or shame. He bought our connection to all the blessings and power of God. He bought our '2nd-chance-forever-pass' that allows us unlimited forgiveness and 'do overs'. He bought all this at the incredible price of His agonizing death and betrayal in front of an angry mob. Having bought this expensive gift, knowing that we could never afford it, He places it on the table before us and says, "*you owe me nothing, I did this just because I love you.*" His economy isn't 'do more, get more', it's 'I did it all, because I love you."

He gave everything. Jesus held nothing back. There was no idea floating in His head that He would offer us 80% of His love, then, if we respond properly, He'll give us the rest, the good stuff. He loves us, because He loves us, because He decided to love us. We're just the undeserving recipients who are invited to receive, but were never asked to pay anything back. God already GAVE HIS BEST to us, freely, no holding back with no return policy ever. He has always been all-in concerning us.

So, my question is, why do we ask for extra prayers when it gets down to the wire for us? What are we secretly saying when we ask for **extra prayers**?

I love this person more than I love other people so I'm asking for Extra prayers please!

I believe this cause is more important than the causes of others so Extra prayers are needed!

Extra prayers needed *because this is really important to me and if I don't get it, I don't know what I'll do!*

It looks like this will be a tough situation to deal with if it goes bad, but I'm sure God will help if we all ask Him, but louder, with tears and really mean it this time. I need your extra prayers!

We may not think we are saying those things but remember observation 2.

God already GAVE HIS BEST to us, freely, no holding back, with no return policy ever.

That means that we don't have to try harder to get more from God. It's all ours already because of Jesus. Let's be wise and careful about how we approach God in prayer. If we know that God can do and wants to do, then let's rest in the fact that He will do! Obviously, being sovereign and omniscient, He may have a better plan than what we are asking for, but we can determine ahead of time that our faith is resting in Him. Resting, not trying harder, resting! Prayer is more for our sake, to reaffirm our trust, bring our heart and mind into focus and give voice against our doubts and fears. Is it possible that when we say 'extra prayers needed' we're actually secretly doubting God's desire and ability to bless?

I hope I have God's attention, but if He's not listening, perhaps extra prayers are needed (*to pull Him out of His apathy toward me*)!

Extra prayers needed *in case God's not feeling up to the challenge today*!

God may have other plans but extra prayers are needed (*to out-vote Him and get what I want*)!

We may not think that is what we are saying, but then why are we asking for extra prayers to get the attention and

166

affection of a God who already gave everything for us and promised everything to us? Shouldn't a broken hearted child of God know that they can fall into the arms of their gentle Father? Could we be falling for a trick, a devilish lie, that God may abandon us if we don't remind Him of what He's supposed to do?

Ask people to pray with you and for your concerns? That's good and the right thing to do. Ask those who have a faith walk that you respect to get involved in praying for the things that need prayer? That is a wondrous tool to calm our fears and encourage our faith. It's vital that we remember to start out from a place of knowing that we already have His best, His all, His love.

As for me, I always picture God with His sleeves rolled up, ready to do His best work in my life, any time I ask Him to.

Remember, we don't have to **try harder** to **get more** from God!

Untitled (just like me)

I am not a Bible scholar or even an expert on being me! I am still discovering everything about anything. I know young people aim at being "*young professionals*" and folks my age often see themselves as experts. I find myself borrowing a line from a TV show, "*I'm more of an ancient amateur.*" The only thing I am greatly experienced with is my own need to change and grow and hold onto Jesus with both hands.

I am a man who sought a title over 30 years ago and still has no professional credentials. I am not a children's director, a youth pastor or a lead teacher. I am a Russ and I am trying to just do what God wants me to do.

So why no title? (*I often ask myself the same question*)

Have I tried to get the title and the job that I think I'm supposed to have? Well, yes I have at times. I went to Bible College for 2 plus years. I've applied several times to churches for the children's director or youth pastor job. I even applied 4 times to the church I currently attend. In each case, I'm not completely sure if I failed, was rejected by the board, blocked by God or just didn't try hard enough. The question is simply; do I have to have the title or job, to do the work? My answer is no and yes. NO because Jesus told 11 fishermen to just go, teach and do the things they saw Him teach and do. That was it, here, you're on the team, go do this and thanks. The answer is also YES, because in this era of church scandal, background checks, law suits and terrified parents, you have to be proven and tried, trained and equipped in order to serve properly. I am an ancient amateur in this field of children's ministry and I am still untitled.

The unrelenting personal questions?
Why would God leave me here, untitled for over 30 years? My honest guess is because He has a lot of other ancient amateurs that need to know that it's ok. Prayer

warriors never trained in the classroom or compassionate councilors tempered only by their own bumpy road. These are people led into a volunteer-career by the love of God in their hearts and not by a text book or accredited school. If I can offer my own journey as a way of saying God loves you and what you do, even if there are no diplomas on your walls and no name plaques on your desks, then so be it. Consider yourself hugged and thanked for being a faithful whatever you are. You and I have the titles that matter the most...

- Dearly loved child of God
- Completely forgiven, new creation
- Sons and daughters of the King
- Redeemed and Holy
- Blessed and hidden in the Beloved

Untitled isn't so bad when you realize you're not alone and not forgotten.

Untitled isn't so bad when you realize your efforts count in eternity, even if they seem to be uncelebrated here.

Untitled isn't so bad when you take a moment and remember you do it for your gentle and wise King who sees it, and appreciates all you do for those that He loves so much!

Don't get me wrong I still struggle at times with my lack of title. My fragile human ego is somehow always tuned to the 24-hour-self-doubt-station. I hear an earthly voice telling me that I have wasted my talents and don't provide for my family as well as I should. Yes I struggle with that stuff too. My eyes see those who are successful professionals at 28, in the field I still volunteer in at 55. I see the conferences they attend and the things they own and the praise they get. At times, it makes my heart hurt.

I MUST CLARIFY that I am deeply loved and appreciated. There are many people that I admire, who treat me with an embarrassing amount of respect and honor. I am fortunate and appreciated, and the other voice in my head screams, "*That should be enough!*" It is, most of the time. It's only when I fall into comparison that my ego becomes the loudest whining voice in my head.

I look forward to the day my King separates me from myself and brings me home. I will be free from the other voices in my heart and head! The 2 greatest joys in eternity will be, being with my Jesus and getting away from 'me'. Only then will all drives, for title and self, be gone and I will gladly sink into the blissful rest of true humility. *Aaahh*, I can't wait.

Why am I talking about this stuff? Does it seem that I'm being a bit whiney? (*I'm glad you asked*)

I want you to know that if you struggle with being untitled, if you feel overlooked, if you feel like a failure because you haven't reached the level of success that you hoped for, it's actually much more normal than you might think. It's quite human to wear those glasses when we look at ourselves but hear this; God declares that you are amazing! There are facts and there is truth. Facts are bits of verifiable information and truth is this giant reality that God has all tangled together and we get to taste parts of it as we walk with Him. Remember, Jesus said He is the way, the TRUTH and the life.

Perhaps it comes down to this, <u>Facts are, information without Jesus and Truth is, Jesus in all our facts!</u>

Jesus walked His road with no degree, no letters of recommendation from the board of trustees, no office with an administrative assistant, just the testimony of what He said and did. Those 'above' Him, in the religious and social sense, did not cheer or applaud His arrival. There were no posters saying, 'Appearing for 3 nights only at our Synagogue!' To the eyes of religion, He was untitled.

Do you know who was titled? An angel named Lucifer. He was called the 'Morning Star' and he had a place of honor and authority in Heaven. Now his titles include 'father of lies', 'accuser of the brethren', 'thief' and 'the wicked one'.

In the end, our words and deeds are our titles. The life we live is the name badge we wear! The Apostle Paul began as an honored and respected teacher of the law, but an enemy of God. His life changed when he was touched by Jesus and his words and actions changed too. Paul referred to himself as "a prisoner of Christ Jesus", in Ephesians 3. His introductions went from "I am Saul and I AM..." to "I am Paul and HE IS." If I can hold onto that everyday, I can also stand against the flesh and failings within me as they scream out my deficiencies.

I am Russ and HE IS MY KING. I am Russ, a servant of the Lord. I am Russ; I am my beloved's and He is mine.

That is a pretty darn good title; **I am my beloved's**.

Vanishing menagerie

I spoke with a gentleman a while ago. Knowing some of the details of this person's story, I was surprised when he told me what his biggest regret in life was. I actually had to ask him to repeat what he said, because I was troubled at the spiritual-heart implications of his statement.

The conversation had begun as we talked about his current home. After a few minutes of discussion, he asked me if I had seen his previous house lately. I said that I had and that I noticed the yard was overgrown and seemed to be full of junk. He shook his head and made this statement, "that's my biggest regret in life, selling that house to him." He was nearly tormented by the condition of the home he once owned. Was his stuff his kingdom? Was his legacy what he had once owned?

Yes, I am being a bit hard and judgmental in this case because I happen to care about this person and am heartbroken for him that his greatest regret isn't about something more important, something a bit more 'eternal'.

I know that his mother was a mean woman and that his dad was kind, but died when this guy was young. I know that he worked hard all his life and gave up a lot of dreams to support his family. I know his job had serious long -term effects on his health. I know that he and his siblings have had several conflicts that kept them from talking to each other for years. What I don't know is why the lawn issue bothered him more than any of that.

Is it possible for us to really put more value on things that fade and decay and slip through our fingers than the lives around us? These collections that perish, these temporal things, this vanishing menagerie!

I thought that a person's biggest regret would be more like...

"I never told my Grandpa that I loved him"
"I still feel bad about that person I hurt when I was younger"
You know, the bad things done or the good things left undone, but not the condition of the yard at the house you once owned! My heart broke for the guy, that his life seemed to be so disconnected from an entire world in need of the joys of love.

I left that conversation thinking about my biggest regrets; the girl who's heart I broke with my selfishness when I was younger, the prostitute that I didn't defend from a self-righteous mob when I was in Bible College, the time I didn't spend cheering for my son when he was young before my divorce, the goofy kid in school that I picked on until he cried.

It's as if our regrets put clear price tags on the things from our past. In a Godly sense, <u>Regret can be a declaration of what we now consider to be precious, that we had previously considered worthless</u>!

May my regrets be more for those people I've hurt and not the lost comic book collection. The love I never shared and not the lawn that goes un-mowed. The difference I could have made in the lives around me and not my vanishing menagerie.

The sound of His voice

(Don't let this one tie up your brain too much, it's just 'some-supposing' I went through)

Sound waves, by definition, are '*the pattern of disturbance caused by the movement of energy traveling through a medium (such as air, water, or any other liquid or solid matter) as it propagates away from the source of the* **sound**. *The source is some object that causes a vibration, such as a ringing telephone, or a person's vocal chords.*'

(Gen 1:1) In the beginning, **God created** the heavens and the earth. (Gen 1:3) and <u>**God said**</u>, Let there be light: ***and there was*** light.

I was recently reading a kids devotional that mixed a bit of science fact with a bit of Bible truth. It had nothing complicated or deep, just enough to keep their attention and plant a little seed. As often happens with me, my brain took a simple classroom concept and ran for the end zone. BAM! Out of the class, past the principal, out the main door and across the street for the athletic field and a touchdown.

The devotion mentioned this fun-fact about astronauts outside of the space ship. They need to use helmets in space that have radios. Radio waves can travel in space, but "<u>sound can't travel in a vacuum</u>." The vibrations of voice require a medium to travel through. Air, water, wood, metal, any of them will work, but a vacuum is death to sound waves.

So, how was God's voice heard in the nothingness before creation? Even after He made the planets, and the air was gathered into the surrounding atmospheres, the space part of the universe had no air to conduct His voice/sound waves. C'mon, am I the only geek with some serious questions here?

I am not questioning the account of creation in the Bible or God's ability at all. I am trying to make the missing pieces fit together in a way that honors the Bible and my God. Often this wild pursuit fills me with a renewed awe for my wondrous creator. Would I be disappointed if there was oxygen everywhere before creation? Of course not, God can tell His story any way that He wants to, but I think there wasn't any air and I think something more fantastical happened!!!

- Was His voice made of something other than sound waves? (*God-waves*)
- Was it made of ALL waves combined? (*sound, radio, light, seismic, electromagnet, thought, emotional...*)
- Was (*or is*) His voice made of MATTER so the vibrations were carried on the very substance of His voice as it came out?
- Was everything He created, <u>made out of the substance of His voice</u> and not just by the authority of it? *Could that be why the heavens declare the glory of God? Because the heavens and the rest of creation have the substance of His voice in them still?*
- Is there something like an eternal membrane between the reality of heaven and the reality of creation, (*like parallel universes in science fiction stories*) and God's voice just pushes through the membrane and is changed from word to matter?
- Was He speaking from heaven (*which had air*) into 'a nothingness' just beyond heaven's borders?

...or, is He so far beyond imagination that none of this even comes close to explaining **what** the voice of creation was really like?

I can't wait to hear and see and taste and feel the sound of His voice. THE VOICE OF MY BELOVED!

Opposite of omniscience

I get a lot of seed thoughts while driving and since I can't write while I drive, I often ask my wife to quickly text me a note to remind me of the thought. I then go on to ask her some odd questions to see if my train of thought is something that others could follow if I wrote about it. That is what happened this time.

We had been discussing an instance of judging another person (*sadly yes, we do this at times*). It made us both sad that we had made a snap judgment about another person because we thought one of their habits was a bit weird. At this point I can no longer remember what the habit was, only that my mind left the conversation for a minute and wandered back to my *'go to'* Bible story for judging. (*Jn 8:1-11 the woman caught in adultery*)

Jesus made it clear that we people have a very selfish and narrow way of viewing life. We see it like we are the star and the whole story revolves around us. We get to pick the heroes and the villains. We should hold the pen that dictates what truth is! In this Bible passage, Jesus could have said, *"Knock it off, you're a bunch of selfish, cry babies and your making me sick!"* But He approached it differently, to make a more powerful point. He said to the men that were accusing this woman of sin, "If you have no sin, go ahead and throw the first stone." In effect, he was saying to them, ***"You are right, she deserves judgment, so whoever DOESN'T deserve judgment should get first shot at killing/judging her."***

We often show our 'awareness' of the things others do wrong! An awareness that is dangerous, since it is limited. Our awareness is limited by our own desire to avoid being judged, so we choose to block our knowledge of our own guilt. It's limited by our inability to see everything, every action, every word and every thought with absolute and impartial clarity. It is also limited because we cannot understand everything that led up to each action or thought of others. We are incapable of knowing the actual motives of any other person and rarely do we even understand our own motives. <u>Jesus pointed this out by refusing to make her sin the topic of conversation.</u> Instead, <u>He made the conversation about the innocence of the men accusing her.</u> In affect he was asking, "Do you know yourselves as well as you say you know her? Are you free from judgment?"

My thoughts brought me next to an obvious statement.

Only the *Omniscience* of God knows all these factors perfectly and can judge justly! (*Omniscience - all knowing, understanding everything seen and the hidden, at the same time*)

Then this popped into my head. "<u>What is the opposite of Omniscience?</u>" *Meaning, what or who, is utterly incapable of making correct judgments.*

I turned to my wife and said, "There is no wrong answer to this question. I just want to see if my train of thought is still running on a track that can be followed. What is the opposite of omniscience?" *She smiled because I do this to her a lot).* She paused about 7 seconds, really considering the question, then turned to me and said, "**US. People are the opposite of omniscience**". I smiled and thanked her for her answer.

How true that the opposite of omniscience is <u>us</u>. Yet we run to make judgments as if it is our right. Without the Holy Spirit, we are nothing more than walking selfish opinions and should really just practice keeping our mouths shut!

Job 40:4-5

From the future you

Hello Russ, I'm sending this letter back in time to you, me, US, when you're 13!

Well, I'm 55 now and I know you won't believe it but, we're doing pretty good and have become a lot more of the person you hoped we'd be. Our 20's or 30's were rough. We made a lot of mistakes. So please be patient with us! God has a plan to take us as far as He can before we die, and He will do just that. He has already seen how many years it will take and planned for it.

That means there is nothing so cruel or embarrassing or bad in your life that He hasn't already forgiven it and dealt with it! LISTEN, it doesn't matter whether it was done to you or you did it your self or to your self. HE TOOK CARE OF IT. Allow your self to forgive and be forgiven! It really makes the journey better.

Love? Glad you asked, YES it's out there and God will take as long as He has to, to get the other person ready for you and you ready for the other person. Don't give up. It will be worth the wait.

Be kind to everyone that you can, so you won't have giant regrets and blame yourself. It's okay to be so nice that other people take advantage of you or think you are a fool. In all truth, people like that may only ever get the kindness in life that you allow them to take from you and that is so sad for them. So don't worry about it, your generosity will plant seeds in good soil too! Don't chase money or career or fame or approval; chase God and truth and love and joy!!!!!!! That's what heroes do. So, if you are on that path, God can let you bump into the right person for you, on the same path.

Believe big, take chances and have the kind of story that will inspire your grandkids to reach for a big God in their lives too. Remember, when this life ends and we are all resting in a perfect Heaven, we won't have any more chances to change the world. We won't have any more chances to take a leap of faith. We won't have any more chances to put others first. This place, life here on earth, is our only chance to stand up to the devil, grab onto our invisible God and make the angels stare at us with their mouths hanging open!

This life is our only chance to put on the cape and fly, while others just shake their heads and say that's impossible, that's crazy.

Most of all, be patient, let God chisel away at all the things that aren't supposed to be part of you and He'll prove to you that YOU are a masterpiece!!! I love you and I will see you later.

Hugs from the future you

They don't sell that there

"Bloom where you're planted?"

If you go into a Chinese food restaurant and ask for a copy of Steven King's newest novel, they will tell you, "<u>you're in the wrong place</u>."

If you go to the bowling alley and ask them for a set of new snow tires, they will say, "<u>we don't sell those here!</u>"

If you go to the gas station with a broken arm and ask them to fix it...... (*well, you get the point*)

We often hear Christians saying this phrase, "*Bloom where you're planted.*" It's supposed to be a sort of encouragement to stick with your crappy situation and be like Jesus, but it often comes across as someone preaching down at you saying *'suck it up and smile, stop complaining'*. There are plenty of verses that give the idea that God can give you joy in any situation and that we don't need to escape a season that is difficult or unpleasant. God is more than enough, as Paul wrote, "*His grace is sufficient for me.*" (*2 Cor 12:9*)

It's this idea of **blooming** that bothers me. To me it implies; big smile, hugs, whistle while you work, laugh it all off. An impossible request when your heart is broken, when hope is running thin and when you're too tired to try anymore. Bloom? Don't tell me to bloom when my German Shepherd dies while I'm out of town. There won't be blooming when my son stops speaking to me or when my wife is heartsick because her Dad dies. God offers comfort, peace and hope in those times. He even offers to carry us when we can't walk through the valley of grief anymore. I don't recall Him telling me to bloom.

Seasons change and they change us too. We grow because of seasons. Just like flowers though, our seasons have different purposes. Some seasons are just about roots reaching down and growing deep, for stability and nourishment. Other seasons are about reaching up, how we stand with God, our spiritual posture. Seasons are set aside for pruning or dealing with weeds or fighting disease. Eventually, we all have seasons of blooming, but even these seasons lead to seasons of scattering seeds or growing healthy fruit. <u>Blooming is a season among many seasons</u> for us as Christ followers. Look at Paul and Peter, they had a lot of un-bloomed seasons in their lives and it was okay. All seasons are for growth, but not all are for blooming and THAT is God's design.

I want to change the phrase to *'Grow and Change where you're planted'*. It is important for us to allow ourselves (*and others*) to be un-bloomed if we need to be. When I think about losing my dog several years ago, it brings immediate tears to my eyes. It makes me miss her and remember her sounds and smells and the way she played with me and always made me feel welcome in our home. I have peace and comfort and a deep thankfulness for God allowing me the times I had with her, but I cry. I cry because of love!

I don't smile and whistle in my seasons of mourning, ...because <u>they don't sell that there</u>!

Mourning is a sacred season full of growth and change. It's ok to put away the smiles and un-bloom for a season. God understands and will meet you there.

In mourning, He sits quietly beside you and gently holds your hand, which is a miracle that we don't usually see, when we're busy blooming!

When Rahab was born

Let me just begin with this, in chapter 1 of Matthew's Gospel, Rahab is mentioned in the lineage of Jesus. She's about 10 generations after Abraham and about 32 before Jesus. Just tossed in the middle there and without a doubt, it is very significant that she is mentioned.

Women had no place of honor in ancient Jewish culture and prostitutes were an unclean disgrace! Yet there she is, related to Jesus. Proclaimed to be in the ancestry of the King of Kings, the Messiah. How embarrassing... how insulting... how beautifully liberating!

Some Bible and Hebrew scholars have said that Rahab was about 30 years old when the walls of Jericho came tumbling down. That means that when Rahab was born, the children of God had left Egypt and were wandering around in the desert for 10 years already. Well, not wandering, more like stalled. According to scholars, the Israelites were kind of parked in a place called Kadesh. It was part of a cleansing process God had for Israel. It was about 38 years of no miracles and no word from God. A hollow spiritual existence waiting for all the men over 20 who marched out of Egypt, to die, so God could start with a new generation.

God was trying to get them to leave their slavery mindset behind and live as free people, but they struggled so much that He had to let that generation pass away so they wouldn't bring their Egypt-emotional-baggage into the Promised Land! It should have only taken about 11 days to walk from Egypt to the Promised Land but it took them 40 years instead. Only Joshua and Caleb were allowed to make it from Egypt to the Promised Land. Yet it was during this cleansing period that in the city of Jericho, a baby girl was born. Her name was Rahab and she would grow up to be a filthy and unacceptable woman, who also happens to be the hero of our story!

Joshua 2-6, is the story of the taking of Jericho. In that story, we first meet Rahab or as she is referred to, 'Rahab the harlot'. Let's be honest here, she was a prostitute, she traded sex for money. She was a woman that would've been declared unclean and a sinner deserving death by the laws of Israel.

This woman of bad reputation was born a precious little girl during the time of Israel's bad reputation, about 30 year's earlier. Some speculate that her prostitution was part of the family culture she was born into and not even her choice, which would explain a few things. How did her word have enough authority in her family, to compel them all to gather at her home for protection? What did the 2 spies see in her that they felt they could trust her promise to keep them hidden and safe? Was this woman a virtuous harlot? Did her eyes and voice and presence convey something much richer and deeper in her soul, than her title implied? I won't know until I get to ask the people involved, but until then, I know that this little baby born during the parked, outcast of Israel, was destined to be a part of Jesus' family tree. An honored part of that tree indeed.

How wondrous and kind it is that the God of Israel, while disciplining His own children, was also looking after a child born to enemies. A child raised as trash, a life full of hurt, and a heart somehow full of hope and honor. A heart waiting for 30 years to recognize a God strong enough to destroy her land and free her life!!! That is what it was going to take for her. Her land, her heritage and her past had to be destroyed. Utterly defeated, so she could be free. Free to be what she knew she was: honorable, clean and worth loving. A woman worth having in the family tree of Jesus.

Thank God He loves His enemies and the children of His enemies, for I was one too.

Attentive listener

Here's my issue.

God doesn't just hand us what we want. We all know that. **But the real problem is that we expect Him to come to the table of prayer with His mind made up about what we need and how He's going to do the stuff He already decided to do. No matter what we want.** It's like we go to Him expecting to not have a voice, a real voice that He '*actually listens to*'.

You know, like at the DMV or Doctor's office when they say 'next' and never look you in the eye or listen to your request? They just bark-out the same questions that they repeat to everyone else that has ever stood in that line. That's a very man-made religious view of God and not an accurate one. I get it though. Our natural mind turns Him into **The Boss of Heaven-Co.** He's in charge and He's going to run it His way. We are surrounded our entire lives by leaders and bosses who treat us like they are doing us a huge favor by allowing us to serve them. THAT is the devil's plan right there. He gives us horrible counterfeits of the things of God! The devil's hate for God and for us, is so twisted and mean, that He gets us to believe that our Heavenly Father is just like our earthly fathers. That God 'manages' us like our bosses or teachers do.

The devil is desperately invested in getting us to believe that God is *'a bully with no interest in us personally, who has an exclusive plan that He will see through, at any cost to us'*. He wants us to complain and not be thankful, shaking our fists in defiance and not helping to make things better. In other words, Satan wants us to be like <u>him</u>.

Jesus, knowing the devil's plan, came to earth to live a life that shows us the real face and heart of God. He humbled Himself. He went to school, did chores and was all together human. He treated others, even those that the 'Jewish leaders' labeled as unclean, as individuals of great worth.

184

He gave value to their voices!

Do we not get pictures in the Bible of how often Jesus allowed people to interrupt Him?

The lame man lowered through the roof by friends; Jesus was interrupted.

The woman with the issue of blood that touched His garment; Jesus was interrupted.

Jairus begging for his daughter's life; Jesus was interrupted.

The Lord often allowed the cries for help to interrupt what He was doing. He knew their actual needs already, but gave value to their voices with His time. He still does that with us.

We should be thankful for a Divine Creator who attentively listens to less-than-divine requests, over and over again, even if our earthly Dad never did. How else would He be able to promise to bottle all our tears? In Ps 56:8 notice that He doesn't qualify and say only tears that line up with His purpose. He bottles all of our tears because He loves His children. Your fits of despair matter to Him. Your sobs of shame matter to Him. It's what love does. It listens with an attentive heart.

Jesus - God with us, hearing us, seeing us and fully knowing us. God. Not just the boss of the universe, but a real friend to you and me.

Always an attentive listener.

Where do you place flairs?

I was thinking about God's plan for His children here on earth. You know, how we have every good thing waiting for us in heaven, so God asks us to relinquish our claim to our days here and just do His will until we get home.

YUP!!! I went FULL COMMITMENT in the first paragraph.

No working up to it, no excuses, just the simple math of the gospel. God promises all of forever, so I give Him my remaining today's here on earth. Simple math, but we're so reluctant to jump there. We find little religious phrases to keep us entangled in this life. "Don't be so heavenly minded that you're no earthly good"... "I'm only human"... "God knows how I am, He made me this way"... and the awful "To thine ownself be true". TRUE????

How about TRUTH? We were created for a purpose. We were bought back from death and now we literally belong to the one who purchased us from the grave.

So our lives have a purpose. We are to be the light in this dark world. But let's figure out a bit more of why. What does light do for the darkness? It chases the darkness away and exposes the truth; the truth of the perils and lies that are hidden in the darkness. They are hidden traps and in the darkness there are also those who are trapped. Those trapped and those headed for the traps.

When there is a car in trouble on the road at night, we use flairs. Flairs mark off the troubled car two ways. It marks it as an obstacle and potential hazard to others on the road. "Watch out! Slow down!! Be careful this area is dangerous!!!" The flairs also act as a protective barrier for the troubled car and it's occupants, "LOOK OUT FOR US! Be careful. Stay away!! Pay attention!!!".

(*Still lost? Sorry about that...*)

What I'm trying to get at is that we are supposed to be God's road flairs in this dark and troubled world. Warn and protect. Warn and protect! Are our words exhortation and encouragement? Jesus healed and defended. He healed kindly and generously. He defended with honor and a fierceness that only comes from love. He was the great road flair.

A woman caught in adultery? He stood between her and the crowd with rocks in their hands.
Burning brightly and protected her.

A tax collector betraying his own people? He invited him out of his lucrative prison, warning this road does not lead to life.
Burning brightly and led him to safety.

Jesus is a road flair to individuals, families, towns and nations, which ever the situation needs. He is our example not just our Savior! We are supposed to follow that example.
(Stay with me...)

We don't <u>have to</u> live like Jesus. We don't <u>have to</u> accept His purpose for our 'bought-back' lives. We don't <u>have to</u> surrender our desires for God's desires.
That is the definition of free will!

It is our God given right and <u>opportunity</u> to serve a purpose much more important than ourselves! We don't <u>have to</u>.
WE GET TO.

You can't do that

I recently saw a picture of a pie with a large triangular piece cut out of the middle. Not the usual wedge from the crust to the center, just a random triangle in the middle of the pie. The person posting the picture was complaining about how wrong and insensitive the culprit was for doing that. I admit that I laughed and thought it was an awesome way to annoy someone.

As weird things often make me do, I thought about the spiritual applications of what I just saw. I guessed at the reactions of people as if they were to come home and see this pie on the table were they left it. Only it now has a piece cut out of it in this highly untraditional way.

"Why would anyone..."
"Who do they think they are to just go and..."
"That's not how you are supposed to..."
"You can't do that, it's just not done that way..."

During the time of the New Testament, I'm sure those same phrases came out of the mouths of a lot of folks who saw how Jesus and the disciples did stuff.

"Why would anyone... waste their time talking to someone like her?"

"Who do they think they are to just go and... heal someone without following the rules?"

"That's not how you are supposed to... interact with those unclean people!"

"You can't do that, it's just not done that way... people have to earn forgiveness from God!"

A friend was recently discussing a remodeling project that a church wanted to do. He was telling me that they sent a man

188

to the zoning office to find out if what they wanted to do was something that they were even allowed to do. It was a very informative conversation. On my way home from the visit, it struck me that we often tell God what He's allowed to do in our lives or in the lives of others. We remind Him of the rules of operation and our expectations of how things should be. If He gets too much work done in someone else's life, we complain about the scheduling in our own. If there's too little visible progress on someone's journey, we tell Him the job isn't cost affective and He should probably quit. We like to be in control. We want to hand out the building permits to God.

<u>God IS the zoning office</u>! God is the architect, planner, builder, landscaper, plumber, electrician, painter, decorator and the project finisher. (*if we let Him be*) It's our choice really, do we let God do what he wants or do we say 'you cant do that, it's just not the way it works'? Sounds silly I know, but we often tell the same God who said, "Sun stand still" or "dry bones come back to life", that he isn't allowed to do things His way. What was the biggest complaint from the religious leaders in Jesus' time? "YOU CAN'T JUST GO AROUND FORGIVING EVERYONE! WHO DO YOU THINK YOU ARE?"

We have to let God be God. Let Him do a miracle if He wants to. C'mon, God can put the cart before the horse... heck, He can put the horse inside the cart and still make it work if He wants to. Jeremiah 17:5 says, "*Thus saith the LORD; Cursed be the man that trusteth in man, and maketh flesh his arm, and whose heart departeth from the LORD.*" I always picture that verse saying that I am cursed if I take away God's power and give Him arms of flesh. If I restrict the power of God in one area, then how have I not also restricted His power to save me?

Let God be God in your own and everyone else's life! He is God and yes, He can do that!!!

God <u>is the zoning office</u>!

How do you know it's broken?

How do we know if something is broken? Is there a warning light? Did pieces fall off? Is it stuck? Does it make a weird sound? I guess we'd all probably have different ways of defining broken. For this conversation let me say that broken means; *not working the way it was intended to work; not functioning the way it was designed to function*. I don't think broken has to mean 'doesn't work at all', just doesn't work properly. (*You know, like a car with a steaming radiator and a wobbly wheel that pulls to the left or a clock that doesn't keep time right*) It sort of works, but it's broken!

I think we all need to be more honest with ourselves. All of us, even kids, need to be encouraged to grab onto this one for insight, honest reflection and Godly self-evaluation.

We all have stuff; things, toys and tools. We know they are broken. We know when they don't exactly do the things they are supposed to do. The problem is that we don't apply this same simple logic to ourselves. We don't look at ourselves and ask what isn't working. Are my choices for friends '*working*' for me or getting me into trouble? <u>Broken</u>. Do my decision-making skills help me get healthy or keep a job or pass my classes or any of the other things they should be doing for me? <u>Broken</u>.
Does my ability to communicate with others make things better or is it <u>BROKEN</u>?

I recently spoke to a young lady who was worried about her mother. She said that her mom has no friends to help her with relocating. This situation made the young lady mad. I know the mother and have seen her on several occasions do things that she knew would push friends away. Without any disrespect, I would say that she often 'un-friended' herself from those she wanted as friends. She could have thought about it and come to the conclusion that her friend making skills were broken.

Now, as I said, I meant no disrespect to those I just wrote about, in fact, we all have situations where our personalities, decisions and lifestyles are broken.

Spiritually speaking, **being broken** is not a sin. It is because of sin, but not a sin itself.
When we yield to it and just live in it, that is sin.

As humans we have this amazingly horrible ability to blame every problem on someone else, instead of examining ourselves to see what isn't working. We do this so we don't have to figure out what it is that's broken about us. For some reason, we find it hard to accept that we will always need God's help, that we need a savior. We deny our own brokenness with the disclaimer, "that's just how I am, I've always been this way" or other phrases like that.
Seriously, think about it. If we have a toaster that takes 3 tries to brown our bagel properly, that sucker goes in the trash and is replaced the next payday! But, if the problem is me... "HEY, people gotta accept me the way I am!"

What's my proof, my confirmation that I am broken and don't work the way I'm supposed to??? I often think mean thoughts about people. I get selfish at times. I don't like to give up my time to help others, when there's something else I want to do. I don't always tell the truth. I have had several unsuccessful relationships. Sometimes I want revenge. I often ignore the needs of others. My ego often gets the best of me and a billion other examples.

Anybody else with me on this?
The weird thing is, when we notice one of our tools, toys or favorite things is broken, we do something about it. Take the car to the shop, buy a new toy, watch a video on repairing it or, compare it to one that works right.

"COMPARE IT TO ONE THAT WORKS RIGHT"

That should be us, comparing ourselves to Jesus, the only human free of sin, unbroken and functioning as He was designed to. So why don't we do that more often? *Compare our selves to Jesus*? We don't like to hear that we've failed or we're broken. I get that, but let's not let just accept the way we are. What we need to see in our comparison to the Lord is that He is always there to help us. See what I mean? We hear I'M BROKEN, when what God is really saying is **I'M ALWAYS HERE TO HELP YOU!**

Ps 46:1 - God is our refuge and strength, a very present help in trouble.

We were made to need God, lean on God and be with God.
Are we functioning like that?
(or are we broken in that too?)

Put that dog down

I pulled up to a traffic light the other day and as I sat there waiting for it to turn green, I glanced to my right where a gas station was. There was a guy walking around his car carrying a small dog. My little smart-alecky inner-voice said, "It's got 4 legs, put the dog down!"

In spite of my rudeness, there was a grain of truth in there. Dogs weren't built to be carried around like a toy. They were given 4 legs and a lot of energy to chase rabbits, catch Frisbees and jump over logs. I realize it's completely acceptable now to walk around carrying a dog, even into a store, because it's a service dog or a comfort dog or just because we want to. We call the pampering 'love'. We even have strollers for them! (*It makes me shake my head*)

We have chosen to take something out of context and make it commonly acceptable in a situation that is ridiculous. (*Not talking about service dogs of course*) Dogs walk and run and scratch and dig and jump and fetch and play and roll and all the other doggy things. They are faster than us by design and a healthy dog has better stamina than we do. Shepherds and farmers use dogs to herd for a reason, they are built for the exercise and many breeds need lots of exercise to stay healthy. But, we decided that they were *cute* and should be carried around like a purse (*or in a purse*) and nobody better say anything to me about it or else. *It's like the story The Emperor's new clothes!*

Ok Russ, where's the spiritual application or is this just an old guy venting?

Christians often 'carry the dog around'. We take something that God intended for a purpose in our lives, flip it around and pull it completely out of context until it no longer bears any fruit. Do you know what kind of things God intends to use to help us grow and mature? Struggle, conflict, waiting, misunderstandings, disagreements and head-butting <u>are all for our benefit</u>. It's life, we are different people with different backgrounds and to have a successful faith-walk, we need to work together, compromise! Compromise means growth and change. It also means becoming understanding of each other and it makes us need God to lead with His Spirit, instead of us leading ourselves with our own opinions and brokenness.

Instead of letting conflicts challenge us into leaning on God for growth and change; we grab them, tuck them under our arms and walk away toward something more convenient. Seasons of struggle are meant to help us change into a more Godly version of ourselves. They have a sacred work to do!

What does this '*dog*' look like in our lives? Do you find yourself annoyed with the lighting at church? The music? The pamphlets or offering buckets? The Pastor's accent or his use of the word *shazam*? The lady who sits behind you every week? The old carpeting? The new chairs? (*we all tend to grumble about something*) Do we want a way out of our annoying church or do we want God to fix that part of us that is so easily annoyed? "Put that dog down!"

Conflict has a purpose. Let God use it to teach you whatever He's trying to teach you.

Romans 5:3-5 says, "*We can rejoice, too, when we run into problems and trials, for we know that they help us develop endurance. And endurance develops strength of character, and character strengthens our confident hope of salvation. And this hope will not lead to disappointment. For we know how dearly God loves us, because he has given us the Holy Spirit to fill our hearts with his love.*"

So don't pick the dog up, that's not what it's built for. God allows problems to help us grow into; better people, better parents, better friends, better married people and better Christians!

Put the dog down and let it do what God made dogs to do.

You're not mine to hurt

I was driving the work van to take a young lady to her doctor appointment. My wife was in the car too and we were all talking about something together and I noticed the face of the young lady turning sad. I wasn't sure what had happened but I figured it was probably one of my comments to her. I often made statements to her that were a bit confrontational to her immature side. I had seen her be very mature and so I held her to a higher standard because of the things I know she was capable of. I also wanted to help her prepare for the very grown up task of being a teen Mom that was before her. However, I never wanted to hurt her in the process.

We still had a little ways to go before we got to the doctor's office, so I left her alone and started thinking of how I would fix my mistake. I was kicking around some thoughts on how to speak kindly and let her know that I was sorry and that it is never my intention to cause emotional bruises to her. As I was looking for the right words and the right spirit with God to talk to her, this phrase popped into my head:

"you're not mine to hurt." (*Meaning that I was acting as a sort of foster parent in my job and I did not have the authority to hurt her with words*)

She wasn't MY daughter. I did love her and wanted the best for her including learning how to represent herself to others. So they would see the wonderful things in her that I see. But, I was only a **'loaner-parent'** and I had no right to expect anything from her or demand anything of her. I certainly had no right to hurt her! Then, the Holy Spirit kind of pulled one of His '*wouldn't that*' questions on me.

"Wouldn't that apply to you and your own kids too?"

"Wouldn't that mean that they were loaner kids from God and I had no right to hurt them either?? Biological/familial connections or not???"

"Wouldn't that then apply to everyone on the planet???? Loaner neighbors, loaner bosses, loaner families, loaner wife, loaner everybody? All people who we (I) have no right to hurt!"

The answer in my heart was YES!

...then this came to me...

What if, before I said a word to anyone, I paused and said in my heart:
"You're not mine to hurt".

What if all my arguments started that way, with me pausing and thinking, *you're not mine to hurt*? What would that look like in my world? What would change inside me? What would change in my outward vocabulary? What (*or who*) would people see in my actions and in my countenance? They'd probably see Jesus -

Jesus, who had the authority to hurt us, but did not.

Why doesn't that work for everybody?

My wife and I were watching the trailer for a Christian movie. The last part of the trailer has the main character saying something like, "my father was a monster and I saw God completely change him." After that scene, my wife asked, "*Why doesn't that work for everybody?*" What she was really asking was, 'why doesn't God answer everyone's prayers like that'?

What a great question, so honest and so sad. The kind of question that a lot of religious people won't ask because it has 'doubt' in it or it has no answer or seems to put God on the spot or worse yet, it points out our utter inability to really understand the workings of an all powerful, all knowing, sovereign God! It leaves us with our hand over our mouths like Job. (*Job 40:1-5*) My wife though, has an extremely honest walk with God and says the things that some churches tell you not to say. She doesn't do it out of pride or arrogance, she just wants to understand the things of God that she doesn't understand. Some of the things we see in the Bible and in life, don't seem to fit the God we have come to know. God is kind to everyone, so why doesn't He answer everyone's prayers the same way?

Let me start answering that by telling you about a different answer I gave once. We had some kids in class that were very bright and wanted their faith to make sense to them personally. They weren't going to settle for living on the faith of their parents. I set up a table and put two cardboard cities on it called Sodom and Gomorrah. I told the kids a bit about the Bible story but then asked them, "Why would a loving God destroy all the people in two entire cities?" I left that question in their laps for a minute. There was silence as they tried to make sense of it.

I then told them about a guy called the 'friend of God'. His name was Abraham. He had the same question for God. God told Abraham He was going to destroy the two cities. Abraham walked with God and asked Him a bunch of questions. "Lord if there are 50 good (*righteous*) people in the cities, will you destroy them too?" God said, "No, I will not destroy the cities if I find 50 righteous people there." This conversation went on until Abraham got all the way down to 'if there are ten righteous people there', and God said, 'I will not destroy the cities if there are ten'.

The beautiful thing about this was that God allowed Abraham to negotiate with Him. God didn't say, "because I said so!" He walked with Abraham so that Abraham could have time to make sense of it. So he could understand how the loving God he knows, could destroy all those people. I told the kids about the conversation between God and Abraham and asked them, "why did Abraham stop at 10?" After a moment or two, one kid said sheepishly, "Because he knew God would do the right thing?" BOOM - Yes, he stopped asking because he finally realized this wasn't something God was going to do to teach them a lesson, it wasn't what He wanted to do, it was something He had to do. God is always kind but He's also always right!

My next question was, "why would this ever be the right thing to do?" I told the kids that there were lots of other people living on the planet too. Why would God wipeout these two cities? "To protect everyone else?", a child asked. Would that be kind and right? The kids all started to talk and agree. To save everyone else from the evil of Sodom and Gomorrah, God might have had to remove them from the earth. "Maybe God knew that the evil of those two cities would spread like a poison across all the other lands and nobody in those two cities would ever want to stop it. Because they liked hurting everyone else."

I asked them, "if this is true, what would be kind and what would be right?" They answered, what God did was right and it was kind for everyone else. I asked them if it still sounded like a mean God, they said no it just sounded sad. I told them it made God sad too.

Back to my earlier question...

I don't know why IT doesn't work for everyone. Why some parents have to bury kids and others don't. Why some people live with broken hearts and others don't. Why drugs rob some families and not others. Why some families love each other and others don't. I don't know and until I see God face to face in heaven, I will never know. I actually CAN'T KNOW until then!!! What I can know is that God is always kind and always right, and I can trust Him.

We are programmed as people to ask for an explanation, to understand, to weigh evidence, to count on logic. God doesn't tell us that there isn't a good reason, He just doesn't tell us what that good reason is. So it's about trust, which means He wants us to know Him. He wants us to talk to Him and listen to him and look for what he is trying to show us. When we get to know God more than we know a religion, we start to trust Him. Not because He says so, but because "I know my Jesus. He is kind and right and good."

There is a portion of scripture that is called the fruit of the spirit, meaning wherever the Spirit of God is moving, these things will grow there. There are nine things listed:

Love - Joy - Peace - Patience - Kindness - Goodness - Faithfulness - Gentleness and Self-control

... As a gardener in our lives, <u>God sometimes has to do some weeding to make room for the good stuff to grow</u>. I have seen God work and have learned to expect His reasons to be kind and right, no matter how it looks to me. Or whatever anyone else says. I know my Jesus, though I've never seen Him. I guess that is exactly what faith is.

Why doesn't it work for everybody? I don't know, but I do know that what God does, is kind and right!

If you are having trouble moving beyond church and religion, into knowing God, just ask Him to bring you to a new place with Him. *Lord, I want to know <u>you</u>, not just know 'about you'. Help me to hear you, help me to see what you show me and help me to be honest with you, as you are honest with me.*

He loves you and wants to be known by you. It's all He ever wanted. That's why He made a place to spend forever with you!

HOPE is my madness

Being an optimist isn't easy for me. It is a <u>necessity</u>. An absolute, gut-wrenching necessity!

There is a sort of murder/mystery movie that I love and it opens with a young man asking a young lady why she believes in God. Her answer is,
"I can't believe in people. I have to believe in something or I'd fall. Fall down through the cracks. Never stop falling."
The movie is sad and it makes me think of my own emotional tar when I lose sight of hope. When I lose sight of all the hope that I have in My Jesus.

Hope, for me, is an every moment thing because the other option is too much for my heart. I see the pain, the wrongs, the hurt, and the poisons of humanity. All the same diseases I find in myself. I see it and it crushes me! Every day I see it, but I also see the hand of God reaching through it everyday as well. Always inviting me, always saying He can show me a different view, always telling me He understands and cares. Always asking me if I will let Him lift me up out of that fog.

I am an optimist because I am also a frightened and overwhelmed little boy reaching for the hand of my kind and gentle Jesus. I reach for it because I have to, to live on this planet! When I take His hand, I can understand and care too. Maybe that's part of being <u>made in His image</u>?
There's a line from the musical "Man of La Mancha" (*based on the book Don Quixote*). Cervantes is in prison being badgered for His fantasies of chivalry. He says, "and the maddest of all, to see life as it is and not as it should be." *- I will come back to that speech a little later. For now, let me change tracks in this conversation*

This train of thought came out of a recent 'fair fight' I had with my wife. A 'fair fight', by my definition, is *when 2 people both communicate their hurts or differences, clearly and honestly.* _Not to win an argument, but to be heard, so that adjustments can be made by both parties and unity can be kept._

My wife had just made a comment that inadvertently knocked the hope out of my hand. So I went for a walk to the mailbox and talked with God about how I felt as I went. OK, I whined and complained! "Why does she... doesn't she know...?" I do that alone with God to get it out of my system. The one thing I must refuse to do is go to her angry and use the words, "you never" or "you always". Those are words you can't take back and those are bitter seeds to scatter in haste!!! Once you say them, you both start making lists of disappointments and that usually wounds any relationship. So, I vent to God and then ask Him to bring wisdom to my tongue and calmness to my heart, before I speak to my wife.

When I got back from my walk, I sat in front of my computer and played a worship song in order to reconnect my heart on the issue at hand. When the song was done, I got ready to go to the store with my wife. We sat in the car and she asked me what was wrong because my face showed some hurt. I explained why I was hurt and the conversation got messy. When there was a break in the discussion, I asked if I could start over and use a different illustration to explain myself. This is what I said:

You know that scene in the movie 'Nacho Libre' where his friend offers him an ear of corn on a stick and Nacho slaps it out of his hand saying, "Get that corn outta my face!" Well, that is how I felt. It was like I was offering some hope to my wife in a small situation and she slapped it out of my hand.

I completely understand that when life is kicking you in the teeth, you often don't want someone to start singing, "the sun will come up tomorrow." (*I do try to exercise wisdom and compassion before dumping my particular brand of sunshine on those who are struggling*) I hope only to ease pain and never dismiss it. People are allowed to struggle and have crappy days. I want to offer a hand up, not tell them that their sorrows are invalid.

The honest truth is that sin has broken <u>everything on this planet</u> and not a single person will ever be free of their sin, until they die.

So, making it through this damaged life is really an issue of **hope**. Hope isn't something we use to combat the reality of life. Hope is what we need in spite of the reality of life. It's the madness we have to choose, to balance out the reality we have to see. *Back to "Man of LaMancha."* The main character has a speech in prison before he gets summoned to the Spanish Inquisition to die.

*"Life as it is. I've lived for over 40 years and I've seen life as it is. Pain. Misery. Cruelty beyond belief. I've heard all the voices of God's noblest creature. Moans from bundles of filth in the street. I've been a soldier and a slave. I've seen my comrades fall in battle or die more slowly under the lash in Africa. I've held them in my arms at the final moment. These were men who saw life as it is, yet they died despairing. No glory, no brave last words, only their eyes, filled with confusion, questioning "Why?" I do not think they were asking why they were dying, but why they had ever lived. When life itself seems lunatic, who knows where madness lies? Perhaps to be too practical is madness; to surrender dreams, this may be madness; to seek treasure where there is only trash. Too much sanity may be madness! **And maddest of all... to see life as it is and not as it should be**!"*

I cry at that every time I watch it.

HOPE is the madness we have to choose. Like something we find in our pockets and offer to someone in need. *"Do you have any change?"* We reach in our pocket, not knowing exactly what's in there, just something, an ounce of hope, a handful of encouragement? No promise to fix anything, just a glimmer of hope. A Godly "what if" or "maybe it will". There are many times I cannot give someone an answer or a promise or a good reason... only a hope. A hope <u>based on the Jesus I have come to know</u>. **My Jesus!** A generous God, a loving Savior an attentive strategist who has planned to redeem everything He can from our sad and broken stories.

What I have to offer in your hurts is merely a hope.

I don't create the hope or even gather it. It shows up. My pockets fill with hope when I walk with Jesus. Just as my swim trunks get sand in the pockets when I swim in the ocean.

When my pockets are empty, I get sad and heartbroken because this madness of hope is much more than what I have to offer others. It is my only lifeline! Everything Jesus has promised me is only fully manifested in heaven. All the trophies of my life here will only be given to me when this life is over. **Until Heaven proves me sane, I live on the madness of hope.** Heb 11:1.

I need my pockets to have hope in them. I need it to give to others and I need it for me. It's the ticket stub for the train ride I can't take yet. I am so thankful that God just gives it to anyone looking for it. He stuffs it in our pockets and puts more in when we give it away. It's intangible, invisible, un-provable and the realist thing I have ever known.

If it truly is madness to try to see with the eyes of a compassionate, invisible God, then so be it. I don't like my other choice! (*Or the me that comes with that choice*)

Until Heaven proves me sane, I live on the madness of hope.

Closing comments

So, that was a brief look into my mind and heart on this journey with my Jesus. I apologize if you need some kind of therapy after reading my '*Devoted Ponderings*'. God has walked me through a lot of changes. Some of them were changes I didn't really want to embrace at the moment, but all of them were for my good. All of them make me a better me. It humbles me to know that He thinks I'm worth walking to the next better version of me. I'm worth upgrading!

That is sort of the underlying theme, *'the changing shouldn't stop'*. Time is given to us for that purpose. We must allow Him continual permission to run His immeasurable self through our hearts and minds for the express purpose of changing us into the image of His son, Jesus. It's hard and frightening. We must consider the bits He might want to chisel out of us. The things He might urge us to volunteer for. Those people we find unlovable that He might ask us to love. The only guarantee change gives, is that we will be different from how we were.

Yet without *change*, we have nothing to offer to a desperate world. Nothing!

Changed though, we can _____ (*fill in the blank*). SERIOUSLY, WE CAN!

John 14:12-*13* *"Very truly I tell you, whoever believes in me will do the works I have been doing, and they will do even greater things than these, because I am going to the Father. And I will do whatever you ask in my name, so that the Father may be glorified in the Son."*

I sincerely thank you for riding my bus. God bless you and may He make your faith and life, impossible to explain without Him.

Hugs, Russ